VOLUME 37

HAWKER
SEA FURY

BY KEV DARLING

specialtypress

PUBLISHERS AND WHOLESALERS

Published by
Specialty Press Publishers and Wholesalers
39966 Grand Avenue
North Branch, MN 55056
United States of America
(800) 895-4585 or (651) 277-1400
http://www.specialtypress.com

Distributed in the UK and Europe by
Midland Publishing
4 Watling Drive
Hinckley LE10 3EY, England
Tel: 01455 233 747 Fax: 01455 233 737
http://www.midlandcountiessuperstore.com

ISBN 1-58007-063-9

Front Cover: *Ellsworth Getchell's FB Mk.11 WH587, N260X, Sea Fury in flight.* (Jim Dunn)
Back Cover (Left Top): *G-BTTA/243 is actually a Sea Fury painted in accurate Iraqi Air Force colors. It was photographed at Yeovilton in 1994.* (C P Russell Smith Collection)
Back Cover (Right Top): *The wing fold on the Sea Fury was hydraulically operated, as was the locking mechanism. Even so, external indicator pins were used to confirm the safety of the outer panels.* (Based on material supplied by the FAAM}
Back Cover (Right Lower): *Although Sea Fury F.10 VR940 is in an undignified position, this mishap shows the flaps and the drop of the arrestor hook.* (W A Harrison Collection)
Title Page: *Being struck down below by its crew, this Sea Fury FB.11 not only sports Korean War stripes, it also has external fuel tanks on the wing center section points, and triple rocket rails under the folding part of the wing.* (Fleet Air Arm Museum)

TABLE OF CONTENTS

HAWKER SEA FURY

INTRODUCTION

The Hawker Sea Fury is a bit of a mystery to most aircraft enthusiasts. If they are knowledgeable about the company and the designs of Sydney Camm, this last Navy fighter is known to them, although in very little detail. Reno racing fanatics are also familiar with the Fury and Sea Fury, but to these lovers of aircraft racing, the Hawker design is an airframe on which to hang the most powerful piston engine possible, complete with matching propeller.

And yet this last great piston design from the Hawker Aircraft Company is much more. In this volume we trace the intertwined development of the Fleet Air Arm and Hawker that would culminate in the Sea Fury. On the way we touch upon biplanes, then the Hurricane, that bastion of the Battle of Britain, which owes much of its content to the Hawker Fury biplane fighter. A quick glimpse at the Tornado and its subsequent development, the troubled Typhoon, follows. At this point the last vestiges left over from the biplane era make their final play. The next stage arrives in the form of the Tempest, a far more refined and stronger Typhoon. From here the story begins to pick up as first the Lightweight Fury makes it appearance. Rejection by the Royal Air Force does not kill the project, as it would have done in the past, for stepping into the breach is the Royal Navy.

The Fleet Air Arm, the airborne force of the Royal Navy, was part of the RAF until just before the war started in 1939. At the end of that global upheaval, the Fleet Air Arm needed a fighter. The Supermarine Seafire had served well, but was very difficult to land on a pitching, twisting carrier deck. Hawker offered the Fleet Air Arm the Fury, navalized as the Sea Fury. It was ideal, with its wide undercarriage, powerful Centaurus engine, and the ability to lift a reasonable amount of weaponry. The FAA was hooked. The Sea Fury Mk.X entered service in the lead in role and would be followed by a considerable quantity of the more potent FB.11. These would be sorely needed over the beaches and hills of Korea, as the forces of the United Nations struggled to stem the Communist tide streaming down from the north. The Sea Fury would cover itself in glory during numerous missions that would culminate in the shooting down of a jet fighter by possibly the fastest piston fighter ever built.

However fame does not last and cannot slow progress. The Sea Fury would retire as the jet age thrust forward. In would come the Westland Wyvern, complete with its turboprop Mamba engine driving a six-bladed contrarotating propeller. It too would see combat service during the Suez crisis of 1956. Then came the real jets, the Supermarine Attacker, wherein dwelt the last vestiges of the Spitfire, and the Hawker Sea Hawk, the last full design by the company for the Royal Navy.

The clarity of this photo reveals much of the detail pertaining to the Hawker Sea Fury. Close attention shows the detail on the inside of the undercarriage doors and the location of the landing lights and rocket rail mounts on the outer wing panels. (C P Russell Smith Collection)

Wearing its initial delivery scheme is this Sea Fury of the Royal Netherlands Navy. The aircraft is parked with its controls unlocked as the slight disarray of the flying controls reveals. (C P Russell Smith Collection)

The Sea Fury did not completely disappear when it departed the Fleet Air Arm. The navies of the Commonwealth obtained examples, as did countries in the Middle and Far East, where they fared less well in confrontations. However, the ones hardest done by were those delivered to Cuba. Ordered by one regime and used by another, they were pawns in a great communist game before finally fading from the scene.

This was not quite the end. A target tug company in Germany acquired a quantity of retired FAA T.Mk. 20s, and with winches attached, they provided target towing services to the West German armed forces. Private owners bought retired examples for display and racing, and in the United States the Fury has became one of the most popular racing machines. And so we leave this mighty fighter dazzling the crowds at Reno or at air displays in the United Kingdom, courtesy of the RNHF, where they will create memories that will last forever.

ACKNOWLEDGMENTS

In compiling this slim tome, I am indebted to the usual suspects. To Peter Russell Smith, for use of his amazing photo collection; to Bill Harrison, for lending me great photos at such short notice; to Nick Challoner, who always has the elusive shot; and to Thomas Genth, for all the great German material.

Before they feel left out, a very special mention must be made of Jerry Shore and his team at the Fleet Air Arm Museum at Yeovilton. Also, special mention must be made of Mario Overall and all at LAAHS.com, for their help with the Cuban Furies, and Damien Burke, for helping with photos at the last moment. Their help and willingness to cooperate are the model that all museums should follow, Thank you gentlemen!

And finally, mention must be made of the team at Specialty Press and my good friend Dennis R. Jenkins, without whom this would be but a pile of typed paper and photographs.

Kev Darling
Wales
2001

This side on view of Sea Fury VX653 clearly shows the detail in the wing root area and the layout of the undercarriage doors and fairings. (C P Russell Smith Collection)

The rainfall that has soaked this Sea Fury has revealed the panel detail and layout on the fuselage and fin. Reflectance in the puddle under the aircraft reveals further airframe detail. (C P Russell Smith Collection)

Although a proper Sea Fury this aircraft wears a semi military scheme and sports a pair of F-86 fuel tanks in its new role as a Reno racer. (C P Russell Smith Collection)

HAWKER AND THE FAA

INTERTWINING THE FIGHTER AND THE FLEET

Hawker is not a name that readily springs to mind when aircraft operated by the Fleet Air Arm are mentioned. Most casual observers will incline toward the names of de Havilland, Fairey Aircraft and Supermarine before looking at the team from Kingston. However a touch of research into the beginnings of the air wing that was created to defend the capital ships of the Royal Navy will reveal that Hawker was there right at the very beginning.

Great Britain's early entry into the world of naval aviation came courtesy of Thomas, later Sir Thomas, Sopwith. His company is famous for providing the Sopwith Camel and the later Pup to the Royal Flying Corps. Sopwith ventured into naval aviation on 2 August 1917, when Squadron Commander E. H. Dunning piloted a Pup onto the gun deck of HMS *Furious*. Although the trials were to end in a crash landing and the death of the pilot, the seeds of naval flying had been sown.

Just prior to the end of World War I, more formal approaches were taken to create ships to carry aircraft, and carrier-capable aircraft. However, this was a very complicated process as the ships were controlled by the Admiralty and the Royal Navy, while the aircraft came under the Air Ministry and the Royal Air Force. This state of affairs resulted from methods employed to create the Royal Air Force on 1 April 1918. Operating squadrons of the Royal Flying Corps were amalgamated with those of the Royal Naval Air

Service to form the new fighting force. This meant that aircraft carriers of the fleet, such as HMS *Argus*, which was commissioned in 1918, would be stocked with aircraft sanctioned by the Air Ministry, using the Royal Air Force contract system.

Under this convoluted process of procurement, a variety of aircraft, were supplied to the Royal Navy. Some were less than suitable, such as the ungainly Blackburn Blackburn, whose role in life was that of observation for the fleet. In contrast, the fighters were far more streamlined and sleeker and had more powerful engines. Many were redesigns of fighters in service with the Royal Air Force, modified for naval service. The more obvious changes included an arrestor hook, strengthened undercarriages, and a overall improvement of the airframe structure. During the 1920s and 1930s aircraft types entering service with the Fleet Air Arm included the Sea Gladiator, developed from the Gloster fighter in use with the Royal Air Force.

Hawker Aircraft, meanwhile, had evolved from the ashes of the Sopwith Aircraft company, which had run into financial difficulty when all contracts for the Camel and Pup had been abruptly canceled. While Sopwith was not the only company suffering this kind of problem, it was one that would bounce back, although under the aegis of Hawker Aircraft.

In the early 1920s a very bright designer named Harry Hawker had formed H.G. Hawker Engineering and had offered to help Thomas Sopwith put his company back into solvency. However, this was not to be, as Sopwith Aircraft would never reemerge, although remortgaging the company's premises did help clear many of the outstanding debts. This was followed by the untimely death of Harry Hawker in an air crash while he was practicing for an air race. It was revealed later that Hawker suffered from a spinal tubercular disease, resulting in a fatal rupture under the excess G

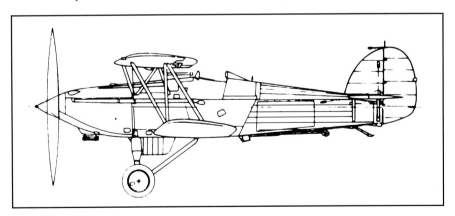

The Hawker Fury was one the fastest and most maneuverable biplanes in RAF service. The Fury and its naval counterpart, the Nimrod, were to lay the foundations for the Hawker Aircraft monoplane fighters. (Big Bird Aviation Collection)

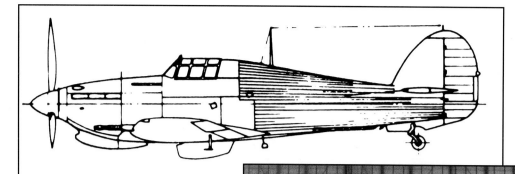

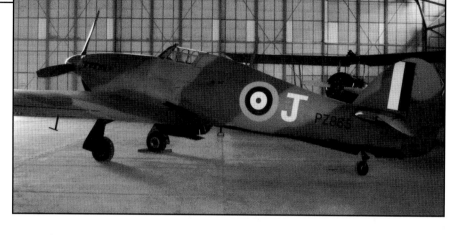

The Sea Hurricane was, like its landborne counterpart, very much a development of the earlier biplanes, as it used similar materials and methods of construction. (Big Bird Aviation Collection)

The Hawker Hurricane was an intermediate stage in the development of the company's fighter program between the early biplane and the more developed fighters that were to follow. (Big Bird Aviation Collection)

forces being exerted upon the man and his machine.

Although the death of Harry Hawker was tragic, it did not mean the demise of Hawker Engineering. With Thomas Sopwith at the helm, the company continued to improve its financial posture, refurbishing aircraft built by other manufacturers and building motorcycles, while it moved closer toward creating an aircraft manufacturing base of its own.

Hawker began producing aircraft under its own name in 1924. In common with others of the period, it was a biplane, as were the many that would follow. The company's first venture into naval aviation was the interestingly named Hawker Hedgehog, a fleet reconnaissance biplane. Although the Hedgehog was unsuccessful in gaining orders, Hawker persevered and won a contract to build a navalized version of the Hawker Fury biplane fighter, then in service with the Royal Air Force.

This new aircraft was slightly more streamlined and lower than its RAF counterpart and was a few miles an hour faster, even though it was

slightly heavier, due to the addition of such items as an arrestor hook. Production versions of the fighter finally joined the fleet in 1932. Other biplanes from Hawker that were to join the fleet squadrons included the Osprey, which introduced folding wings for easier storage below deck.

Seven years later, World War II started and Hawker was fully employed building the Hurricane multigun fighter. The Hurricane was a logical development of the earlier Fury biplane and featured a similar method of construction, utilizing a tubular steel skeleton covered by doped and stretched fabric. Changes otherwise were fairly obvious, including the installation of the Rolls Royce Merlin engine and a retractable undercarriage. It was also during this period, just prior to the events of September 1939, that full control of naval aircraft procurement was finally wrested from the control of the RAF and placed in Admiralty hands.

Naval versions of the successful Hurricane, not unsurprisingly known as the Sea Hurricane, were first postulated for the Catapult Armed Merchantmen or CAM ships. These use-once-only fighters were launched to counter any serious airborne threat to a convoy. Such a defense required abandoning the Hurricane and swiftly rescuing the pilot from the icy sea. A more conventional form of Hurricane operation was undertaken in May 1940, when No. 46 Squadron operated standard aircraft from the deck of HMS *Glorious* in the defense of Norway. Both takeoffs and landings were performed from the carrier without incident, although such interventions did little to stop the fall of Norway.

Development of the Hurricane for the naval role continued, although efforts were angled more toward carrier operations. The first conversions complete with catapult spools and arrestor hooks were entered for test-

ing at Farnborough in March 1941, and later that year, the Sea Hurricane Mk.IB entered service. These were operated from converted merchantmen with flight decks capable of supporting takeoffs and landings.

Further rebuilds of ex-RAF aircraft continued, so that most convoys being escorted to Russia and other destinations had some form of recoverable air defense carried aboard converted merchantmen and purpose-built escort carriers. As the original aircraft carried aboard aircraft carriers had been biplanes, the Sea Hurricane was seen as a major

step forward. The Sea Hurricane remained in front line use with the Home Fleet until replaced by the Supermarine Seafire in late 1943; in the Far East, some examples remained in use until hostilities ended in the region.

After the Hurricane, the Hawker Aircraft Company turned away from producing naval aircraft and concentrated on new fighters for the Royal Air Force. The tubular steel and fabric covering of the wings and fuselage was replaced by sheet metal over a stressed airframe structure. The greatest changes in the

new aircraft from Hawker concerned the fuselage, where the original method of assembly was replaced by a stressed all-metal monocoque structure.

These new designs first surfaced in the abortive Hawker Tornado, which started flying in 1939. Power plants for this aircraft were the Napier Sabre and Rolls-Royce Vulture, both of which were very much experimental at that time. Much of the structure resembled that of the earlier Hurricane, especially the thick chord wings, which were capable of housing 12 machine guns. Although test flying was mainly successful, problems with both engine types hampered development. The Vulture was causing more problems, primarily connecting rods breaking under stress. In light of these faults, the Ministry of Aircraft Production canceled the Vulture to allow Rolls-Royce to concentrate on the much-needed Merlin.

The Hawker Tornado was a development of the Hurricane and was designed as a heavy fighter. However, it never entered RAF service, but was used as a testbed for various engines, including the Centaurus version shown here.
(Big Bird Aviation Collection)

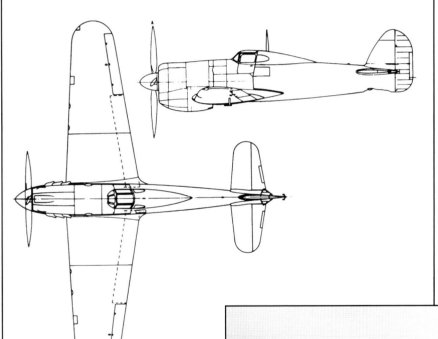

After the Hurricane, Hawker developed the Tornado. This eventually led to the development of the Typhoon, which was intended to mount the Bristol Centaurus although this never happened. This is a Napier Sabre-powered aircraft. Some of the ideas that were to appear in the Sea Fury are already in place, such as the retractable tailwheel.
(C P Russell Smith Collection)

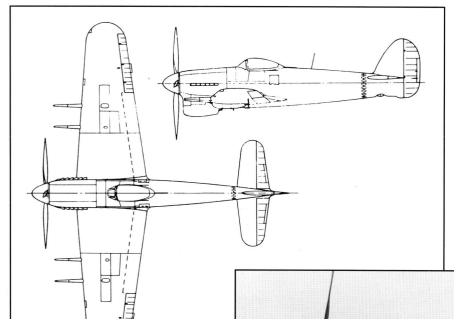

The next stage in the development of a fighter for the RAF was the Typhoon. After initial teething troubles, the Typhoon became a rock-solid ground attack aircraft. (Big Bird Aviation Collection)

The Typhoon 1B eventually became a good ground attack aircraft, a purpose for which it had a quartet of Hispano cannons installed. By the time the Sea Fury came along, all the problems with the cannon installation had been ironed out. (C P Russell Smith Collection)

The Tornado was only produced in small numbers, and was looked on mainly as a stepping stone to other types and as a test and development aircraft. The main powerplant under consideration continued to be the Napier Sabre, which was tested with a variety of propellers, including the standard three-bladed assembly built with different materials and gear ratios. Different configurations were also tested, including four and five blades plus a six-bladed contrarotating assembly.

Other engines also started to feature in the Tornado's lexicon. The new air-cooled 18-cylinder Bristol Centaurus engine had first been proposed for installation by Hawker Chief Designer Sidney Camm in January 1940. Construction of a dedicated prototype was authorized in April of that year, although the airframe was not a completely new one. In fact, only a new center fuselage was required, as parts already available on the Langley production line were used to complete HG641.

Once the aircraft was completed, a Centaurus CE 45 engine was installed, and in October 1941, this new combination undertook its maiden flight. Early test flights revealed a problem with engine cooling, which required a complete redesign of the cowling to cure. Other alterations included relocating the oil cooler as an integral part of the cowling lower surface, while the three-bladed Rotol propeller assembly now sported a large spinner. With the new cowling installed, the Centaurus Tornado was vastly improved in behavior and performance, and a greater priority was given to developing the type.

Priorities, however, changed as Typhoon production came on stream, and the Tornado program was canceled. However, the Centaurus Tornado HG641 continued as a testbed for both the engine and various propeller assemblies, such as the four-bladed unit from Rotol.

The Tornado's immediate successor designed by Sidney Camm was the Typhoon. The engine developed for the Typhoon was a continuance of the Napier Sabre, while the airframe was a combination of the tubular framework of the Hurricane covered by a stressed skin. Also carried over from the Hurricane and the Tornado were the thick chord wings, which were seen from the outset as responsible for the high drag coefficient. Even so, the Napier engine was powerful enough to pull the Typhoon through the sky at a reasonable speed.

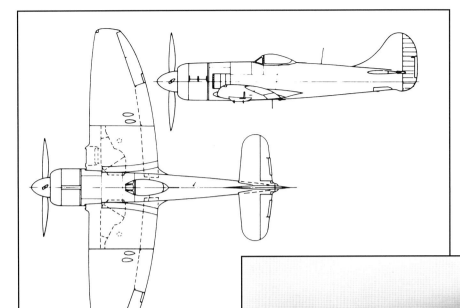

Following on from the Typhoon was the far more refined Tempest. This is the Centaurus-powered Tempest II. (Big Bird Aviation Collection)

The first manifestation of the Hawker Tempest was powered by the Napier Sabre engine. Unlike its predecessor, the Typhoon, the Tempest benefited from a redesigned wing. (C P Russell Smith Collection)

However, a hidden but serious structural problem was to plague the early aircraft. The tail unit attachment to the rear fuselage developed an annoying habit of detaching itself in flight. mainly under extreme handling conditions. Once the cause had been determined, Hawker undertook an extensive modification program.

While the Typhoon was going through its tribulations, the Hawker design team was looking at developing an aircraft from the Centaurus powered Tornado. This was to be a radical departure from the earlier Tornado and Typhoon lineage, and although the new aircraft would look superficially the same, it would be a completely new design. The fuselage would be of a similar outline, but there the similarity ended; the underlying structure would be a fully monocoque design, complete with frames and stringers.

The original wing of the Typhoon had been designed with a NACA 22 series wing, which had a thickness

chord ratio of 18 percent. Although this was more than adequate for the Typhoon in its ground attack role, any further evolution would require a complete redesign as the original had a tendency to induce aileron reversal and suffer severe buffeting in a dive above 500 mph. This had a marked tendency to throw the aim of the guns out of alignment. To counter this, Camm and the rest of the Hawker design team, in consultation with the Directorate of Technical Development, began looking at a completely new layout in which the thickness chord ratio was reduced to 14.5 percent. This decreased to 10 percent at the tip with the thickest point being at the 37.5 percent point. The shape also changed from the earlier rounded planform to be more elliptical in outline.

The new design, originally named the Typhoon II, was tendered to the Air Ministry for consideration. Given the problems encountered by the Typhoon, Hawker was most surprised to be presented with a contract for six prototypes to Specification F.10/41, dated for November 1941. Not long after this, the new aircraft was renamed the Tempest, and the six prototypes were more clearly defined. Two were to be fitted with different versions of the Napier Sabre, two with Rolls-Royce Griffons, and the final pair with Bristol Centaurus engines. In order that the new fighter could begin test flying as quickly as possible, the first prototype featured parts culled from the Typhoon production line, including the tail unit and cockpit assembly. The Hawker Aircraft Company

The Tempest II was powered by the Bristol Centaurus engine, although this was coupled to a four-bladed propeller, rather than the later five-bladed assembly. Many of the features that would appear in the Fury Lightweight Fighter are already in place. (Big Bird Aviation Collection)

gave this project the internal designation of P.1012, which was originally used for a Typhoon II with leading edge radiators.

In a similar vein to the Typhoon, the prototype was prone to a certain instability, which was cured by the addition of a dorsal fin fillet and an increase in the span of the tailplane. On the production aircraft, a slight lengthening of the fuselage was required, as was a redesign of the tail unit assembly itself. Further changes were wrought upon the wing leading edge, where cooling radiators were installed in intakes at the wing roots.

The evolution of the Centaurus-powered Tempest had begun with the Tornado, which in turn had been followed by a single Typhoon, LA594. The Typhoon had not been completed, as the experience gained with the Tornado had been deemed enough for evaluation purposes. In consequence, two Centaurus-powered Tempests, LA602 and LA607, were ordered to develop the type. The first to fly, in June 1942, was LA602, which featured a rigidly mounted Bristol Centaurus. Soon

after the flight test program had begun, the rigid mountings were suspected of causing vibration troubles, although further analysis pointed to an imbalance in the propeller. This was subsequently replaced by a five-bladed unit, though the change seemed to make little difference to the behavior of the engine. A further investigation

now looked closely at the engine mounts, the original stiff items being replaced by six rubber block mounting units, the proposed Dynafocal mountings being delayed until further notice. These coupled with a Rotol four-bladed wooden propeller seemed to cure the problem, and the test program resumed. The second prototype, LA607, also joined the flight test program in September 1943. Both airframes were used in flight trials of the Centaurus IV, V, VII, XII, XV and XVIII. The success of the prototypes in developing the various Centaurus engines led to large orders for the type.

The Hawker Tempest, although a successful aircraft, was seen as big and heavy for many of the fighter roles, such as point defense interception. However, in order to retain as much of the Tempest as possible, Hawker proposed a lightweight version. First moves toward creating the new fighter had begun in September 1943. The original proposal

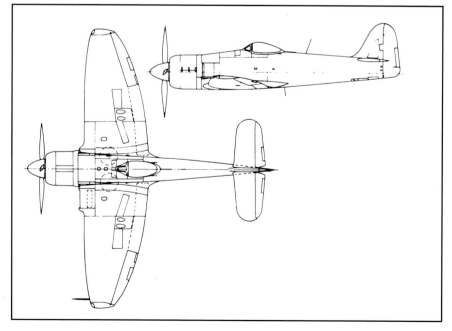

By substantially reducing the wing center section and refining the fuselage, the Lightweight Fury fighter was created for the RAF. While it was not required for this service, the FAA expressed a strong interest. (Big Bird Aviation Collection)

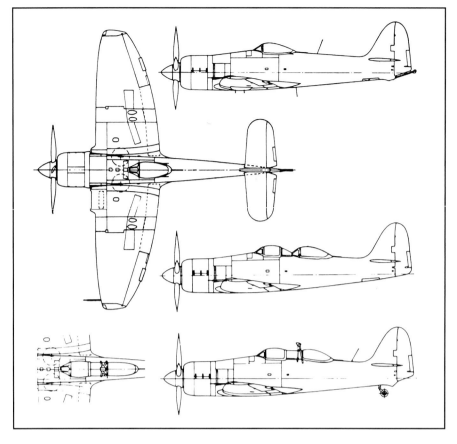

Eventually the Tempest evolved into the Fury Lightweight Fighter and then on to the Sea Fury, as displayed in this general arrangement. The Sea Fury eventually spawned a trainer version. The middle side view is the Iraqi double canopy version, while the lower is the standard T.Mk.20. (Big Bird Aviation Collection)

was centered upon removing the wing center section, thus bringing the two outer wing panels closer to the fuselage. Formalization of the project began in January 1943 with the issuance of Specification F.6/42, which named the resulting aircraft the Tempest Light Weight Fighter (Centaurus). Further refinement of the design led to the Ministry of Supply producing another specification, F.2/43.

In April 1943, on the heels of F.2/43, came a specification to Hawker from the Admiralty for a fighter based on the same aircraft which was defined by N.7/43. To consolidate the design work needed to create both aircraft, Sidney Camm proposed that a single set of requirements be issued to cover the needs of both services under the F.2/43 proposal. Supplementary sheets could be issued for the naval changes required. This would result

in an aircraft powered by a Bristol Centaurus XII engine, with Hawker responsible for the drawings and the Royal Air Force batches. The Royal Navy Fleet Air Arm requirements were to be met by Boulton Paul Aircraft, based at Wolverhampton.

As the Bristol Centaurus was a popular engine, alternative power plants were considered, and by December 1943, six F.2/43 prototypes were on order. Two would have Rolls-Royce Griffons installed; two were to have the Bristol Centaurus XXIIs; one would have a Centaurus XII; and the remaining airframe would be used as a structural test specimen. A further modification to the naval specification resulted in the Admiralty producing N.22/43. For internal identification purposes, Hawker applied the following designations: P.1018, 1019, and 1020 were all allocated to the Fury program and covered the installation of the Napier Sabre IV, Rolls-Royce Griffon 61 and the Bristol Centaurus.

The maiden flight of the first aircraft, NX798, to Specification F.2/43 was undertaken on 1 September 1944 with test pilot Philip Lucas at the controls. The installed power

The first Sea Fury Mk.X was a modified version of the Lightweight Fighter. This airframe featured an arrestor hook but lacked the folding wings of the production version. (C P Russell Smith Collection)

Sea Fury prototype SR661 was fairly close to the first production version, the Mk.X. When this airframe emerged it was powered by a Centaurus 18, driving a four-bladed propeller. Unusually for a naval prototype, this aircraft sports a temperate fighter scheme. (Fleet Air Arm Museum)

plant was the Bristol Centaurus XII although this was replaced later in the flight test program by a Centaurus XVIII. The next evaluation aircraft to fly was LA610, which undertook its first flight on 27 November 1944. This airframe was powered by a Rolls-Royce Griffon, driving a Rotol six-blade contrarotating propeller. Within this time frame the aircraft had finally gained a name. The Royal Air Force version became known as the Fury, and the Fleet Air Arm version was known as the Naval Fury, although this soon changed to Sea Fury.

As the war on all fronts was progressing well from the Allies' point of view, it was inevitable that some aircraft contracts would be canceled. Given that the Royal Air Force had extensive contracts outstanding for various versions of the Spitfire and that many of the Hawker Tempests were delivered into storage, it was unavoidable that such a new and untried fighter as the Fury would be quickly canceled. Although the Royal Air Force pulled out of the Fury program, development of the naval version was set to continue. The fighters deployed on the fleet and light carriers of the Royal Navy

were the Supermarine Seafire and the Fairey Firefly, plus numerous lend-lease aircraft, mainly from the Grumman stable. In the case of the Seafire, the narrow undercarriage track was a known problem, but the aircraft had been chosen for its pure fighter qualities. On the other hand, the Fairey Firefly was seen as a long-range fleet defense fighter, although it was soon adapted to other roles. The main problem with retaining the lend-lease aircraft from the United States centered on purchase costs and spares support. Obviously the Admiralty was keen to replace the American aircraft with those of British origin and to ensure that its carrier decks would not remain bare. Thus the choice fell on the Hawker Naval Fury as the successor.

Although the Royal Air Force had pulled out of the Hawker Fury program, two further prototypes were completed for development work. The first of these, NX802, powered by a Bristol Centaurus XII, made its maiden flight on 27 July 1945. The second airframe, VP207, was completed in 1947 and made its first flight in that same year. The power plant installed in this airframe was the Napier Sabre VII. During its test

flights, this particular aircraft achieved a top speed of 485 mph in level flight, making this the fastest piston fighter ever constructed by Hawker Aircraft. The Fury airframes would continue their test flights as the program split into two distinct sectors. The first of these would be the aircraft for the Fleet Air Arm, the Sea Fury, while the other would encompass development of the type for the export market.

Technical specifications for the Fury, with comparison data for both the Centaurus-powered Tornado and Tempest, are as follows. The span for the Fury was a nominal 38 feet 4 inches, which compares to that of the Tempest at 41 feet, and that of the Tornado at 41 feet 11 inches. Wing area was 283 square feet for the Tornado, 302 square feet for the Tempest, II, and 280 square feet for the Fury. Fuselage length was 34 feet inches while that of the Tempest was 34 feet 5 inches. The Tornado was set at 32 feet 10 inches. Speeds achieved by all three Centaurus powered types were 460 mph at 18,000 feet for the Fury, 442 mph at 15,000 feet for the Tempest, and 402 mph at 18,000 feet for the Tornado. The engines installed in all three types were consecutive developments of the Bristol Centaurus series and were manufactured at the company's Filton, Bristol, plant. That for the Tornado was the type CE 45 rated at 2,210 hp, while the Tempest II had either the Centaurus V or VI, both rated at 2,520 hp. The engine fitted to the Sea Fury series was the 2,480-hp Centaurus XVIII which was an uprated version of the earlier Centaurus XII. The propellers fitted to all three Centaurus powered aircraft were of Rotol Propellers Limited origin, and featured either four-, five-, or six-bladed contrarotating assemblies.

Although the Royal Air Force had canceled its participation in the Hawker Fury program, the Fleet Air Arm remained involved. Even this had its downside, however, as the Admiralty was also in the process of reducing its aircraft requirements. This was to result in the Sea Fury contracts being cut to a total of 100 airframes. The change in emphasis also resulted in the Sea Fury program being returned to the Kingston works of Hawker Aircraft instead of remaining with Boulton Paul Aircraft at Wolverhampton. Also transferred from Boulton Paul was the partially completed prototype VB857, which was trucked to its new home in January 1945.

The delay in completing this airframe meant that the first of the genre to fly was SR661, which took to the air on 21 February 1945. During May 1945, flight trials of this aircraft were undertaken at RAE Farnborough to assess the behavior of the rudder under carrier operating conditions. The assigned pilot commented that the power of the engine needed to be counteracted by extensive deflection of the rudder to starboard. Problems with the handling were exacerbated by a lack of feel, which was compounded by the fitted spring tab, which would eventually lead to tyro pilots mishandling the aircraft. This behavior could be

Photographed while undergoing trials at A&AEE is SR666, showing its wing fully folded. Note the tiedown points on the main undercarriage legs.
(W.A. Harrison Collection)

made even more pronounced if full left rudder was applied before the takeoff run began. As soon as air pressure was applied to the rudder, the powerful spring tab immediately began to compensate, inducing the aircraft to swing to the left.

This would then be compensated for by correcting in the other direction, although this quite frequently occurred just as the Bristol Centaurus engine was reaching full power. Further complications would arise if 30 degrees of flap were set for takeoff.

Powered by a Bristol Centaurus XII engine driving a Rotol four-bladed propeller assembly, this first Sea Fury was a fixed wing machine, but

was fitted with an arrestor hook for deck landing trials. The second prototype, SR666, was more advanced as it featured folding wings, in addition to the already-installed arrestor equipment. However, unlike on later airframes, the original folding mechanism on SR666 was manually operated and locked. This aircraft made its maiden flight on 12 October 1945 and was powered by a Centaurus XV instead of the proposed Centaurus XXII, which had been delayed by production difficulties. In a change from the first prototype, the Rotol propeller assembly was of the five-bladed variety. A third airframe, VB857, was completed in late 1945, making its first flight on 21 January 1946. In common with SR666 this airframe was fully navalized.

The Sea Fury Mk.X prototype SR666 was powered by a Bristol Centaurus engine, which drove a five-bladed propeller assembly. (W A Harrison Collection)

With three airframes available, flight testing of the new type from Kingston was able to begin almost immediately. However, problems began almost summarily with the Centaurus engines, as they had developed a disturbing habit of breaking crankshafts. This was eventually traced to the crankshaft lubrication system, which was found to operate intermittently. The shaft would overheat and break under the shear load. Quite a few pilots found themselves walking home to the test airfield at Langley after the engine had failed, but fortunately there were no casualties.

The final cure to the engine seizure problem was the replacement of the original Centaurus with the definitive engine from Bristols, the Centaurus 18. Much of the development work on this engine was carried out using the F.2/43 prototype, NX802. Once confidence had been restored in the Centaurus engine, seagoing trials on board a carrier could begin. Prior to that however, flight testing had been carried out at the A&AEE at Boscombe Down in 1946 using SR666. After these tests had been completed, the trials process was repeated aboard the aircraft carrier HMS *Victorious*.

These flights concentrated on rudder handling when undertaking carrier landings or practicing missed approaches. During these maneu-

This side view of SR666 clearly reveals the location of the pitot head on the wing and the original short tail hook. (W A Harrison Collection)

Sea Fury TF946 waits for its next pilot. As this is a production machine, it features the extended arrestor hook. (W A Harrison Collection)

vers, the rudder only remained effective using maximum climbing power, although use of full power left the surface ineffective.

Investigations into directional instability during the landing run were also looked at, as the Sea Fury's rudder became totally ineffective on touch down. To compensate for this, harsh aggressive use of the wheel brakes was needed to keep the aircraft traveling in a straight line. A recommendation for a tail wheel lock was put forward and was adopted for production aircraft. The installation of this lock also improved the retraction behavior of the tail wheel unit, which had a tendency to remain off center and would not retract.

Handling in the stall also gave rise to concern, as the ailerons lost full authority at 98 mph in landing configuration; in contrast, the elevators were effective down to 88 mph under the same conditions. Further

faults that appeared during the flight trials concerning the Centaurus engine, still carried on rigid mountings. Once the power had dropped below 1,700 rpm, serious vibration occurred and continued throughout the landing approach. Coupled to this was a tendency for the propeller to overspeed, especially if a go round or emergency throttle was suddenly applied. Eventually the proposed Dynafocal mountings would be introduced, these would help damp any vibration tendencies.

Flight testing of the prototypes had revealed further minor handling problems, and the first prototype was returned to Hawker for rectification. On 5 July 1945 prototype SR661 was returned to the RAE for further evaluation. Changes to this aircraft included the fitment of a five-bladed Rotol propeller, a redesigned rudder assembly, and the airscrew reduction gear altered to a ratio of 0.44. These alterations were greeted with pleasure by the test

pilots, as it improved the rudder control during the most difficult phases of flight. Also improved was the takeoff distance, and in the opposite direction, the five-bladed propeller increased the braking effect upon the aircraft. Coupled to this was an improved undercarriage, which had lost some of its stiffness. This resulted in a far safer deck landing, lacking the uncontrolled bounce of the earlier airframes.

Arrestor hook tests occupied the early part of July and involved exerting loads up to 3 Gs on both the aircraft and pilot, as the aircraft was offset by some 15 feet from the flight deck centerline on each touch down. There were a few missed and bounced wires during this period, so the Sea Fury was returned to Hawkers at Langley for modification to the hook damper mechanism. This was carried out very quickly, and the aircraft returning to RAE Farnborough on 27 July. The modification was approved by the end of the

SR666 is mounted on restraining trestles while it undergoes gun butt firing trials and gun harmonization. (W A Harrison Collection)

month.

Actual deck landing trials for the Sea Fury began on 10 August aboard HMS *Ocean* and were judged successful. Further carrier trials, to be undertaken at Farnborough in July 1946 using SR666, centered on behavior of the Sea Fury during a catapult launch. The aircraft was launched from the land-based catapult in the tail-down, hold-back position. The forces generated by these trials were so great that the tail wheel assembly collapsed under a load of 2.2 Gs. As the runway at Farnborough was asphalt, the damaged fighter was flown to the Hawker airfield at Langley, where a grass landing strip would be gentler to the aircraft. Investigation of the incident revealed that the unlocked tail wheel was shimmying, increasing the already great load upon that assembly. To enable the trials to continue a temporary tail leg was installed, locked in the down position. With the leg in this condition, the maximum speed was held at 200 mph. Although the tail leg limited top speed, the modification allowed acceleration trials to proceed rapidly, and they were completed by the first week in October.

Unlike most other British carrier-borne aircraft, the Sea Fury was equipped with a single centrally mounted carrier launch spool, hence the need for the locking tail wheel. Other carrier aircraft built for the Fleet Air Arm featured two spools spaced farther apart.

In March 1947 the folding wing Sea Fury Mk.X was already in production for the squadrons of the Fleet Air Arm. The fourth production airframe, TF989, was delivered to Farnborough for catapult acceleration trials. Once the trials were completed, the aircraft was transferred to HMS *Illustrious* to evaluate its behavior during takeoff and landing under all conditions. A further sequence of trials were carried out aboard the same aircraft carrier using the sixth production aircraft, Sea Fury TF990. In contrast to the prototypes and the first few production Sea Fury Mk.X, this airframe featured a new type of longer, more rigid arrestor hook. The modified hook made the aircraft far more stable after connecting with the arrestor wire. This airframe upgrade had been as a consequence of problems experienced using the shorter, less rigid hook, which had been the subject of a report from the Intensive Service Trials Unit.

Further trials involving the Sea Fury Mk.X were undertaken using VR920 at Farnborough during November and December 1947. These were

Prototype T.Mk.20 VX818, which had been diverted from the Iraqi ITS order, sits in a mixture of primer and unpainted metal. Unlike the production versions, the prototype was fitted with an arrestor hook. (W A Harrison Collection)

mainly centered on the behavior of external loads, which included weaponry and the RATOG fitments. Although the RATOG gear behaved properly, the same could not be said of the underwing rocket projectiles. As manufactured, the mounting shear pins often failed under the high G loading of off-center arrested landings. Fortunately, the warheads of the rocket projectiles were inert, as they skidded across the deck on touchdown. It was to take the agencies concerned some 11 months to correct this fault.

Although trials were ongoing, so was Sea Fury production. Only 50 of the first version, designated the Mk.X, were ordered. These were virtually identical to prototype SR666 except that the power plant was a 2,480-hp Centaurus 18, which in turn drove a four-bladed propeller. After roll-out, the first production machine, TF895, undertook its maiden flight on 30 September 1946 from the Hawker airfield at Langley, piloted by R.V. Morrell. Of the 50 aircraft manufactured, at least 20 were used for trials work of one kind or another. Hawker Aircraft retained airframes TF895 and TF897 for general performance and handling trials, while TF900 was involved with spring tab trials. Weapons trials were the province of TF923 while airframes TF898 and TF899 were involved with carrier deck landing trials. Preservice release trials were undertaken at A&AEE Boscombe Down, using TF902 and TF908.

Armament trials, involving both the internally mounted Hispano cannons and external loads, was undertaken at Boscombe Down. The 20mm cannons fitted to the Sea Fury were the short-barrel Hispano Mk.V. All four plus ammunition tanks were installed in the wings of the Sea

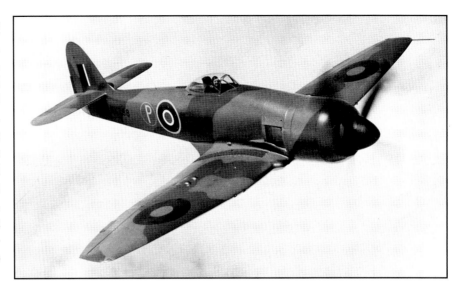

Fury Lightweight Fighter NX798, oriented more toward service with the Royal Air Force, lacked any navalization features. (Fleet Air Arm Museum)

Fury. In addition to the rocket projectiles eventually cleared for service use, of which 16 could be mounted, the prototype SR666 was used to clear both 500 lb. and 1,000 lb. bombs for carriage by the type. Other weapons that were cleared for in-service use included 1,000 lb. incendiary bombs, Type 2 Mk.II smoke floats, and 90-gallon wing-mounted drop tanks. Further trials involving TF923 at Boscombe Down covered the behavior of napalm tanks and their impact when dropped from various heights. Completion of these

trials allowed the Controller Aircraft to clear the Hawker Sea Fury Mk.X for operational use on 31 July 1947.

This clearance allowed Hawker to commence deliveries to the Fleet Air Arm, with No. 778 Squadron equipping in February 1947. Its primary purpose was to act as the training unit, although initially it only received three aircraft, TF905, TF906, and TF907. This strength was quickly reduced when TF906 was lost in a crash on 20 June, its cause being determined as pilot

Sea Fury FB.11 VX853, parked with its canopy fully open. Unlike most aircraft, this machine appears to have its lower footstep retracted. (W A Harrison Collection)

The Sea Fury T.Mk.20 was built with the fairing for the arrestor hook. Although these were not installed on the trainer version, most of the features of the fighter were present. (W A Harrison Collection)

mishandling. The first operational unit to equip with the Sea Fury Mk.X was No. 807 Squadron, based at Eglinton, where in September 1947, the Sea Fury replaced the earlier and more docile Supermarine Seafire Mk.XVII. This contrast in aircraft types was exemplified by the loss of TF915 on 21 August 1948, which crashed on landing when the pilot braked too heavily.

Once Hawker Aircraft had worked the kinks out of Sea Fury Mk.X the company was able to offer the Admiralty the far more capable Sea Fury Mk.11, which was to feature the addition of powered folding wings. The incorporation of this feature enabled the deck crews to strike down the aircraft quickly upon landing. To enable this to be done in the quickest possible time, the wing-fold mechanism was hydraulically powered with locking pins being pushed into position by similar means. All of the weapons that had been cleared for the earlier Mk.X were swiftly released to service for the Mk.11. Fitted as standard to the Sea Fury Mk.11 was the five-bladed Rotol pro-

peller assembly, driven by an 18-cylinder Bristol Centaurus 18 rated at 2,480 hp. The addition of the wing fold mechanism raised the basic weight of the aircraft to 9,240 lb.

With the advent of the new version of the Sea Fury into the service of the Fleet Air Arm, there were changes to the way the aircraft was operated and deployed. This was due to the introduction of the Supermarine Seafire FR.47 into service. As the Sea Fury normally flew with external fuel tanks, its duties were changed to that of fighter bomber, while the shorter ranged Seafire was redefined as a fleet defense fighter. Production of the Sea Fury was spread over a period of seven years and encompassed 615 airframes built at the Hawker plant at Kingston. In May 1948, No. 802 Squadron, based at Eglinton, became the first unit to equip with the Sea Fury. It was soon followed by Nos. 801, 804, 805 and 807 Squadrons, which received their aircraft in March 1951, July 1949, August 1948, and February 1948 respectively. These

four units were to embark on the fleet light carriers HMS *Ocean, Theseus,* and *Glory* for shakedown cruises during 1949 to 1951.

Unlike the normal ordering and development process that frequently surrounds the two-seat trainer buying process, the introduction of a two-seater Sea Fury came after the deal to build a similar version had been completed for Iraq. The first airframe was diverted to the Admiralty upon completion and rolled out to Admiralty Standards of Preparation as VX818. It was first flown from the Hawker test field at Langley on 15 January 1948. After completing company test flying, the aircraft was delivered to the A&AEE Boscombe Down for preservice evaluation. It was during these flights that a weakness was found in the rear canopy, which had collapsed under pressure. Modifications to correct this fault included a completely redesigned cockpit canopy, which saw the insertion of a Perspex tunnel between the cockpits, creating a long glass house. To enable the instructor seated in the back to closely monitor the student in front, a periscope mounted on a frame was installed above the tunnel. To compensate for the changed weights and balances, two of the Hispano cannons were deleted. In contrast to their fighter counterparts, the Sea Fury T.Mk. 20s were not equipped with arrestor hooks and were therefore prohibited from carrier operations. They were, however, fully plumbed to carry external fuel tanks and weapons loads.

Overall a total of 60 Sea Fury T.Mk. 20 trainers were constructed for the Fleet Air Arm. They began to enter service in mid-1950 at Royal Naval Air Station Anthorn, and deliveries continued until March 1952.

Skin and Bones

To better understand the performance and behavior of the Hawker Sea Fury, a review of its construction is essential. The fuselage, built to absorb the stresses and strains of a carrier landing, was constructed in three sections that were bolted together at the transport joints. Each individual section had numerous frames that were held together by numerous stringers, all of which were covered by a stressed alloy skin. Bolted to the rear bulkhead of the fuselage was the tail unit assembly, upon which was mounted the elevators and the rudder. Mounted in the lower rear fuselage was the resettable tail hook, surrounded by reinforced structure. Just forward of the arrestor hook was the retractable tail wheel and its covering doors. The tail wheel unit was equipped with a locking mechanism to improve stability; it retracted forward upon selection.

The Bristol Centaurus engine was mounted on the forward bulkhead, and was encased in cowling panels, which were mounted between the single cowling ring and the fuselage. Reinforcing straps were mounted at intermediate points around this circumference. Exhausting of the 18-cylinder Centaurus power plant was via cut outs in each side of the fuselage. As the gases generated by the engine were extremely hot, the surrounding area was covered and reinforced with a Monel-based alloy. Although the Monel shielding was effective in deflecting the heat from the fuselage, the plates and their mounts were subject to cracking. This required their removal for welding at regular intervals. Mounted on the engine drive shaft was a five-bladed 35-degree offset constant speed propeller unit. A Hobson/ RAE fuel injector pump and the two-speed supercharger were also mounted close to the engine.

Construction of the Sea Fury's wings was very similar in both the Mk. X and Mk. 11, both being constructed with fore and aft spars, there being breaks for wing folding. Mounted close to the wing break points were the main undercarriage units, whose wide track gave the Sea Fury great stability in landing and ground movement. Hydraulic jacks were used to retract and extend these units, while the main fairing doors were mounted to the legs. The upper, smaller hinged doors were mounted to the legs via turnbarrels, which allowed them to slide into place upon retraction. To cover the wheels after they were safely locked in the wheel bays, Hawker provided a triangular fairing door which moved into position via a series of links and bell cranks. Also mounted within the inner section of the wing were the four Hispano 20mm cannons, with their ammunition boxes and guidance tracks. In the Sea Fury Mk. X they were located in the same position. In contrast, the T.Mk. 20 only sported two of these weapons. Covering all was an alloy skin of varying thickness, which was riveted to the spars, ribs, and stringers. Located in the inner wing on the leading edge were intakes that pro-

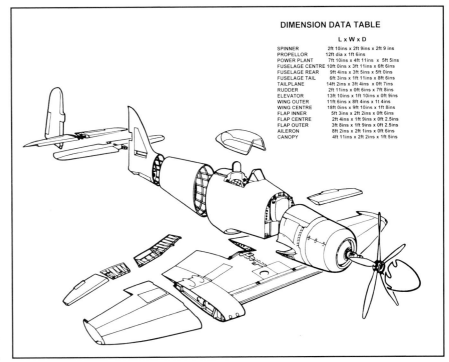

DIMENSION DATA TABLE

L x W x D

SPINNER	2ft 10ins x 2ft 9ins x 2ft 9 ins
PROPELLOR	12ft dia x 1ft 6ins
POWER PLANT	7ft 10ins x 4ft 11ins x 5ft 5ins
FUSELAGE CENTRE	10ft 0ins x 3ft 11ins x 6ft 6ins
FUSELAGE REAR	9ft 4ins x 3ft 5ins x 5ft 0ins
FUSELAGE TAIL	6ft 3ins x 1ft 11ins x 8ft 6ins
TAILPLANE	14ft 2ins x 3ft 4ins x 0ft 7ins
RUDDER	2ft 11ins x 0ft 6ins x 7ft 8ins
ELEVATOR	13ft 10ins x 1ft 10ins x 0ft 9ins
WING OUTER	11ft 6ins x 8ft 4ins x 1ft 4ins
WING CENTRE	18ft 0ins x 9ft 10ins x 1ft 8ins
FLAP INNER	5ft 3ins x 2ft 2ins x 0ft 6ins
FLAP CENTRE	2ft 4ins x 1ft 9ins x 0ft 2.5ins
FLAP OUTER	3ft 8ins x 1ft 9ins x 0ft 2.5ins
AILERON	8ft 2ins x 2ft 1ins x 0ft 6ins
CANOPY	4ft 11ins x 2ft 2ins x 1ft 5ins

The Sea Fury was built in sections, and this diagram was issued to show the dimensions of each item. (Based on material supplied by the FAAM)

vided cooling air to the engine radiators and the oil cooler. Ducting from these intakes led along the front of the undercarriage bays to the engine compartment.

Hydraulics were used to drive the main and tail undercarriage units and the flaps. These were deployed in four sections, with two under the wing inner panels and the others under the wing outer sections. On the Mk. 11 and T.Mk. 20, hydraulics drove the wing fold mechanism and locking pins. This system was also used to extend and lower the tail hook. Damping of this and the main and tail undercarriage units was achieved by the use of air oil dampers, which controlled the oscillations of these items. The pump that drove these systems was engine mounted and provided a constant pressure of 1,800 psi. In the event of an engine-driven pump failure, a hand pump was mounted to the left of the pilot's seat which could drive all these systems, albeit slower and at a reduced pressure. Also driven by an engine gear box was a pneumatic pump, which maintained a charge of 450 to 470 psi in a dedicated cylinder. Under normal requirements, this system operated the brakes, adding the undercarriage and flap emergency blow downs to its repertoire when needed. This feature was not available on the Mk. X, in which the air supply operated the brakes and

This is the rear of the Centaurus engine. As this is a preserved example, the various components can be seen clearly. (Big Bird Aviation Collection)

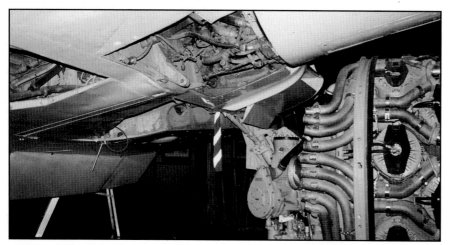

This photo shows the mass of pipework that leads to the engine mounting bulkhead. The couplings for the engine connections are on the other side of this same fireproof bulkhead. (Big Bird Aviation Collection)

This preserved and remarkably clean Centaurus engine shows the layout of the front of the powerplant and the splining on the propeller shaft. (Big Bird Aviation Collection)

undercarriage assisters. Indication was via a triple pressure gauge in the bottom right corner of the instrument panel.

Electrical supplies were courtesy of an engine-driven generator that not only charged the aircraft's two onboard batteries, but powered the lighting, air intake shutter filters, and bomb and rocket projectile controls. Also using this source of energy were the engine cooling shutter controls, engine instruments, fuel booster pump and contents gauges, plus the oil cooler shutters. Gun firing and associated cameras were also electrically powered, as were the gyro gunsight, pressure head heater, radio, and compass.

The fuel system installed in all versions of the Sea Fury consisted of five self-sealing tanks, two in the rear fuselage and the other three in the wings. Two of the wing tanks were interspar tanks, while the other was described as a nose tank, and was located in the starboard wing's leading edge. Although described as two separate fuel tanks, those in the fuselage were interconnected and acted more as one main tank. Fuel feed to the engine was courtesy of a Hobson/RAE injector pump, fuel from the other three tanks was fed to the main tank courtesy of the air pressure supplied from the exhaust side of the vacuum pump. The main tank was not pressurized, fuel flow

The right side of the Centaurus reveals the bank of exhaust pipes and the location of the spark plugs. (Big Bird Aviation Collection)

The left side of the Centaurus. (Big Bird Aviation Collection)

Sea Fury FB.11 VX652 with its wings folded. Although no fuel tanks are fitted, the aircraft does sport a full plethora of rocket rails. (W A Harrison Collection)

from the wing tanks. The main fuel tank contained a total of 97 gallons, while the two interspar tanks contained 56 gallons each. The auxiliary tank held a maximum of 30 gallons, while the nose tank in the right wing had a maximum load of 17 gallons. To extend the range of the Sea Fury, two types of external tank were available, rated at either 45 or 90 gallons. Fuel transfer into the main system was achieved by the same method of air pressure from the vacuum pump. In case of emergency or clearing the wings for combat maneuverability, the underwing tanks could be jettisoned by a lever in the cockpit.

being controlled by a main fuel cock. To prevent overfilling of the system, the main tank incorporated a float valve that shut off supply at the appropriate point. When the contents of the interconnected main fuel tank fell below 117 gallons, the float valve opened and fuel was fed in

To simplify operation of the fuel system, the use of isolation cocks for individual tanks was eliminated,

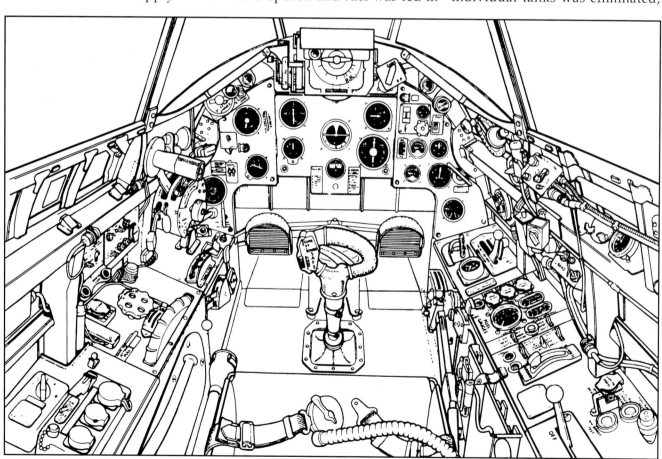

All the dials and controls that assisted the pilot in flying the aircraft and carrying out his mission are visible in this interesting perspective of a Sea Fury cockpit. (Based on material supplied by the FAAM)

and the whole system was regarded as a single group. However, a small measure of control was possible when the wing tanks were involved. When the underwing overload tanks were manually selected, feed from the wing tanks was isolated, and pressure was vented to the atmosphere. In the opposite direction, the wing tanks would supply fuel to the main system while the underwing tanks vented to the atmosphere. On the downside, inadvertent selection of the underwing tanks when they were not installed would shut off the wing tanks. To ensure that this did not occur, a locking lever was fitted when the wings were clean.

Engine starting was assisted by an electrically driven fuel booster pump located in the main fuel tank, although this did not cut in under the automatic system until the engine oil pressure reached 30 psi. This system was subjected to two main modifications. The first, Mod 309, incorporated a manual control that had to be moved to the "on" position before flight and to the "off" position as soon as possible after landing. The second modification, N.22, added a high-pressure pump to the electrical priming pump. This modification provided external priming of the cylinders by a connection in the port wheel bay, which allowed highly volatile fuel to be injected directly. If the electrical pump failed for any reason, fuel supply to the engine would be maintained by the injector pump.

To assist the pilot, the fuel system had four contents gauges that covered the main, interspar, and nose tanks, which were controlled by the ground/flight selector switch. To consolidate these readings, a Pacitor-type main fuel tank gauge was fitted in the pilot's panel. This

gauge had the quirky habit of not reading correctly for at least 30 seconds, while the dedicated power unit warmed up. Fuel contents gauging for the underwing overload tanks was a matter of guesswork, as no indicators were provided. To further assist the pilot in managing the aircraft's fuel contents, a fuel low warning light, located by the main gauge, activated at 107 gallons. By this time, the wing and drop tanks were empty. In addition to the contents gauging system, an air pressure system gauge indicated a correct pressure between 3.25 and 5 psi. If air pres-

sure dropped below 3.25, it could cause problems with fuel transfer at higher altitudes.

Lubrication was as essential to the Bristol Centaurus as to any other engine for efficient operation. The Sea Fury's oil tank, situated in the engine bay forward of the fireproof bulkhead, had a fluid capacity of 14 gallons with an air space of four gallons. The lubrication system incorporated a negative G valve to maintain pressure even when fully inverted, keeping the engine fully operational under all circumstances. To combat the heat generat-

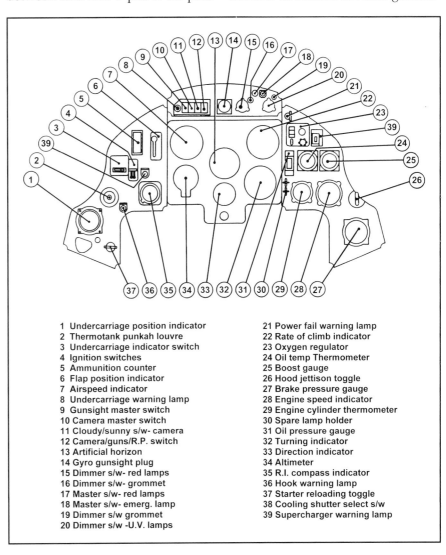

1 Undercarriage position indicator
2 Thermotank punkah louvre
3 Undercarriage indicator switch
4 Ignition switches
5 Ammunition counter
6 Flap position indicator
7 Airspeed indicator
8 Undercarriage warning lamp
9 Gunsight master switch
10 Camera master switch
11 Cloudy/sunny s/w- camera
12 Camera/guns/R.P. switch
13 Artificial horizon
14 Gyro gunsight plug
15 Dimmer s/w- red lamps
16 Dimmer s/w- grommet
17 Master s/w- red lamps
18 Master s/w- emerg. lamp
19 Dimmer s/w grommet
20 Dimmer s/w -U.V. lamps

21 Power fail warning lamp
22 Rate of climb indicator
23 Oxygen regulator
24 Oil temp Thermometer
25 Boost gauge
26 Hood jettison toggle
27 Brake pressure gauge
28 Engine speed indicator
29 Engine cylinder thermometer
30 Spare lamp holder
31 Oil pressure gauge
32 Turning indicator
33 Direction indicator
34 Altimeter
35 R.I. compass indicator
36 Hook warning lamp
37 Starter reloading toggle
38 Cooling shutter select s/w
39 Supercharger warning lamp

This diagram of the pilot's panel shows the location of the primary instruments and most important switches. (Based on material supplied by the FAAM)

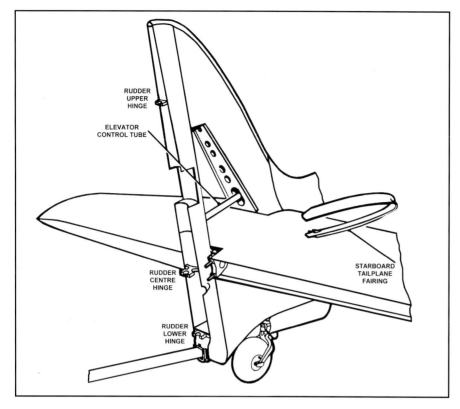

RUDDER
UPPER
HINGE

ELEVATOR
CONTROL TUBE

RUDDER
CENTRE
HINGE

STARBOARD
TAILPLANE
FAIRING

RUDDER
LOWER
HINGE

Many aircraft have the tailplane fitted under the fin. In the case of the Sea Fury, the tailplane assembly was slid through the fin gap for mounting purposes. (Based on material supplied by the FAAM)

ed by the engine and collected by the oil, a cooling intake was located in the port wing root. Operation of this system, including control of the thermostatically controlled electric jack, was fully automatic.

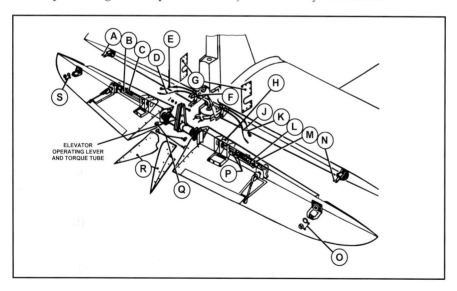

ELEVATOR
OPERATING LEVER
AND TORQUE TUBE

Once the tailplane was refitted, the elevators were attached. On the outer faces, they were mounted on a conventional bearing hinge, while the inners were mounted on a torque tube to which the surfaces and operating lever were also attached. (Based on material supplied by the FAAM)

In contrast to some of the more advanced systems incorporated into the Sea Fury, the flight controls were fairly conventional. Most of their operation was by rods, cables, and bell cranks, with tensioning by adjustable turnbarrels. Operation of the controls in the cockpit was by a spade grip control column, which incorporated the brake lever and gun firing control. This switch also operated the cine camera, released the bombs, and fired the rocket projectiles. The rudder could be adjusted to accommodate pilots of various heights by the use of a centrally located rudder bar adjuster wheel. The pilot's seat was also adjustable vertically, for the same reason. As an airframe can be susceptible to damage if the control surfaces are free in a high wind, there was a stowable locking kit in the cockpit. This consisted of a clip, which mounted on the control column with cables attached to the rudder pedals and to the seat. To protect the ailerons, there were external locking plates specially designed to fit the Sea Fury. These plates were inserted in the gap between the flying surface and the wing structure. This particular method was required, as the operation of the ailerons was controlled by the fitted spring tabs, and not the surfaces themselves.

In contrast to the aileron tabs, those attached to the rudder and elevators were conventional in operation. To assist the pilot in controlling the aircraft, the flight control surfaces had trim tabs fitted. Those of the rudder and elevator were grouped together in a control box in the cockpit. The tab control wheels and indicators were the only items visible to the pilot, the remainder of the control runs being hidden from view. In contrast to the in-flight adjustable trim tabs, those attached to the ailerons

could only be adjusted on the ground. Although the undercarriage system was hydraulically operated, it was activated mechanically. Selection of either "up" or "down" was achieved by the operation of a quadrant selector in the cockpit, with a safety catch to stop inadvertent selection in either direction. This came complete with a warning that "up" should not be selected, as there was a possibility that a ground crew member could push up the cockpit access footstep without realizing that the gear and step were interconnected, thus causing a malfunction in the retraction sequence. Visual indication of the undercarriage position was shown in the cockpit by a sequence of lights on the pilot's panel. In transit, there were three red indicator lights, while in the fully up and locked position, the lights were out. Fully down and locked, the indicator lights were green.

In the event of a green light failure, a secondary set of lights was available, controlled by a pull switch in the center of the indicator panel. For night flying, a twist of the same knob reduced the glare of the lights. As this was the period in aircraft development when electrics were not always trusted, each main undercarriage leg had a mechanical indicator rod fitted. When the gear was down and locked, the rod extended through the wing skin, a useful adjunct, should a malfunctioning microswitch show the opposite. Other indicator lights tied in with the undercarriage locking system included a red light that would come on if the throttle lever should be less than one-third advanced and the gear is not locked down. The other indicator light was interconnected with the port gear leg, and came into play when the gear and the arrestor hook were down and locked.

The FB.11 was capable of utilizing the RATOG launch system. The FB.11 had the RATOG launch units mounted under the wing center section, unlike other aircraft types, which had them above the wing root. (W A Harrison Collection)

Operation of the arrestor hook was by a lever in the cockpit. This, however, was a one-way operation in the air, as the hook could not be retracted once lowered. To aid the pilot, there was a green indicator light on the port side of the cockpit. The landing flaps use an indicator gauge, rather than a light. Operated by a preselector lever in the cockpit, these hydraulically operated surfaces had four predesignated positions—"up," "takeoff," "max lift," and "down," although they could be placed in any position between these stations for better control if needed.

In contrast to the hydraulically operated systems, the Sea Fury wheel brakes were pneumatically powered. A storage cylinder, charged at 450 to 475 psi, provided operating

WG603 is an FB.11 allocated to No. 738 Squadron based at Lee on Solent. Not only did it sport underwing rocket rails, it was also fitted with external fuel tanks. (C P Russell Smith Collection)

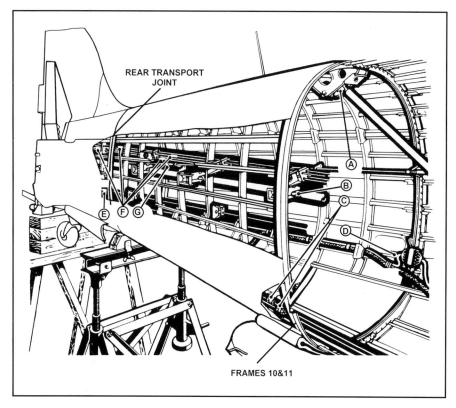

REAR TRANSPORT JOINT

FRAMES 10&11

The construction of the rear fuselage was fairly conventional, consisting of frames and stringers over which was riveted an alloy skin. (Based on material supplied by the FAAM)

pressure for the brake system. Each unit required a maximum of 110 psi. Ground parking was available via a catch, and differential braking was via a valve on the rudder bar.

By the time Hawker started building the Sea Fury FB.11, the confidence in hydraulically operated wing folding and locking was fully established.

Those of the Sea Fury FB.11 and T.20 were operated by a lever in the cockpit, which activated the selector valves, and which in turn allowed fluid to the required side of the jacks. As there could be a conflict between the position of the flaps and the wing outer panels, a safety catch was built into the lever to stop the wings spreading if the flaps were still

down. To keep the pilot exercised, the hand pump could be used to move the wing panels, should there be a problem with the engine-driven pump. This was also a useful adjunct for the ground crew in its servicing operations. As a visual sign that the wings were fully spread and the locks were fully home, indicator rods lay flush, and were exposed when the locks were withdrawn.

In contrast, most of the engine controls were mechanical, and some were automatic. The first of these was the engine mixture control, governed by the throttle lever. The best setting for economical mixture strength was achieved when the throttle setting was at 2,500 rpm with the rpm lever in the auto position. This lever had another position, indicated by the "maximum" label near the quadrant. When the maximum selection was made, engine rpm was increased to 2,700 rpm for short periods. A friction damper, integrated with the rpm control, also applied to the throttle lever. Supporting the more mechanical items engaged in engine control was a fuel cut-off control, which had two settings. One was "normal," while the other was unsurprisingly labeled "cut-off." This control had to be set to the latter setting before the injector and cylinder priming push-

Surrounded by a profusion of rockets, bombs, and fuel tanks, FB.11 VX642 was caught on display in 1948. During the Korean war, the twin rocket mount was found to be damaging the wing structures. (W A Harrison Collection)

WARBIRD**TECH**
S E R I E S

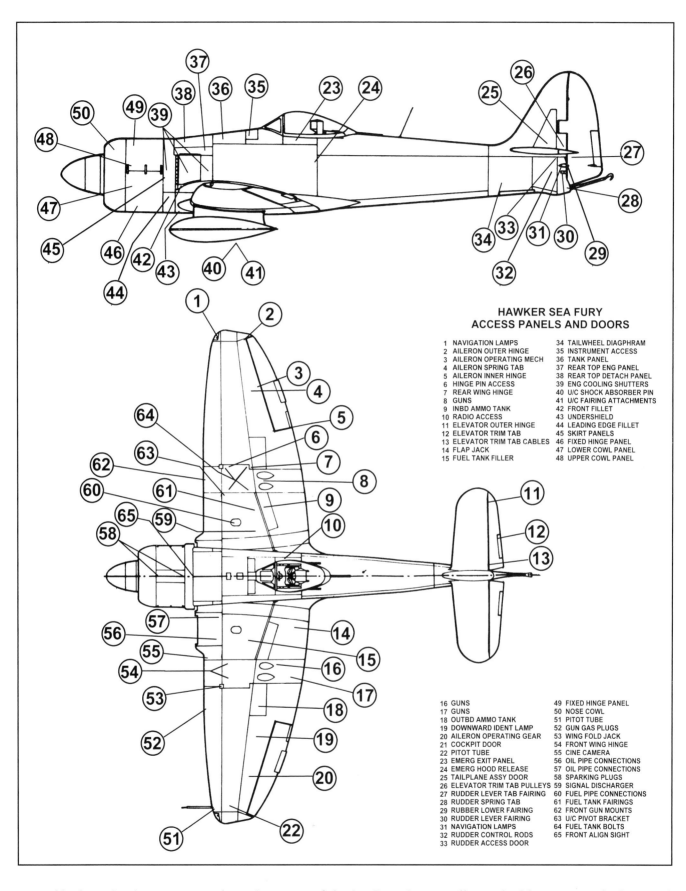

HAWKER SEA FURY
ACCESS PANELS AND DOORS

1	NAVIGATION LAMPS	34	TAILWHEEL DIAGPHRAM
2	AILERON OUTER HINGE	35	INSTRUMENT ACCESS
3	AILERON OPERATING MECH	36	TANK PANEL
4	AILERON SPRING TAB	37	REAR TOP ENG PANEL
5	AILERON INNER HINGE	38	REAR TOP DETACH PANEL
6	HINGE PIN ACCESS	39	ENG COOLING SHUTTERS
7	REAR WING HINGE	40	U/C SHOCK ABSORBER PIN
8	GUNS	41	U/C FAIRING ATTACHMENTS
9	INBD AMMO TANK	42	FRONT FILLET
10	RADIO ACCESS	43	UNDERSHIELD
11	ELEVATOR OUTER HINGE	44	LEADING EDGE FILLET
12	ELEVATOR TRIM TAB	45	SKIRT PANELS
13	ELEVATOR TRIM TAB CABLES	46	FIXED HINGE PANEL
14	FLAP JACK	47	LOWER COWL PANEL
15	FUEL TANK FILLER	48	UPPER COWL PANEL

16	GUNS	49	FIXED HINGE PANEL
17	GUNS	50	NOSE COWL
18	OUTBD AMMO TANK	51	PITOT TUBE
19	DOWNWARD IDENT LAMP	52	GUN GAS PLUGS
20	AILERON OPERATING GEAR	53	WING FOLD JACK
21	COCKPIT DOOR	54	FRONT WING HINGE
22	PITOT TUBE	55	CINE CAMERA
23	EMERG EXIT PANEL	56	OIL PIPE CONNECTIONS
24	EMERG HOOD RELEASE	57	OIL PIPE CONNECTIONS
25	TAILPLANE ASSY DOOR	58	SPARKING PLUGS
26	ELEVATOR TRIM TAB PULLEYS	59	SIGNAL DISCHARGER
27	RUDDER LEVER TAB FAIRING	60	FUEL PIPE CONNECTIONS
28	RUDDER SPRING TAB	61	FUEL TANK FAIRINGS
29	RUBBER LOWER FAIRING	62	FRONT GUN MOUNTS
30	RUDDER LEVER FAIRING	63	U/C PIVOT BRACKET
31	NAVIGATION LAMPS	64	FUEL TANK BOLTS
32	RUDDER CONTROL RODS	65	FRONT ALIGN SIGHT
33	RUDDER ACCESS DOOR		

To enable the maintainers to access the various areas of the Sea Fury, it was well served with access panels. (Big Bird Aviation/Based on material supplied by the FAAM)

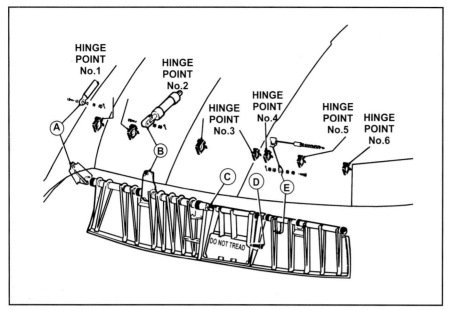

The flaps were conventional in construction and were operated hydraulically. (Based on material supplied by the FAAM)

buttons would engage. As the Bristol Centaurus engine was equipped with a supercharger, there were controls in the cockpit to change the settings, which were (M) low and (S) high gear. To protect the supercharger, a warning light on the pilot's panel came on when the supercharger was engaged in high gear below 7,000 feet.

Further engine and ancillary controls covered the air intake filter, which supplied filtered engine air to the engine. To ensure this worked correctly, the wing root intakes were automatically blanked off. To keep the engine warm at altitude or in cold climes, a warm air control directed warm air to the wing root intakes. Further controls operated and could override the engine cowling shutters; their default position was fully open for takeoff, and they were closed in all other conditions of flight. If at any time a pilot was unsure of the position of the cowling shutters, a quick open selection would trim the nose into the down position.

From this angle, the construction of the flap can clearly be seen. (Big Bird Aviation Collection)

Engine starting was a fairly simple affair, with a pair of ignition switches on the left side of the pilot's panel. This was backed up by a combined cartridge starter and booster coil push button on the opposite side of the cockpit, close by the priming push-buttons. In the event of a misfire, a reset toggle repositioned the Coffman starter breech.

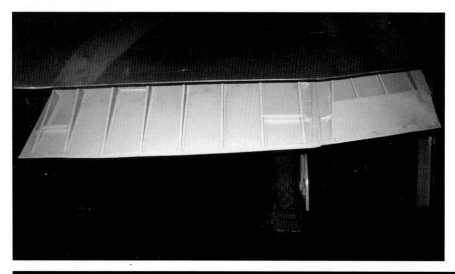

When the flaps are in the down position, it means that wings cannot be lowered, otherwise damage could occur.
(Big Bird Aviation Collection)

Further controls in the cockpit covered other operations. One of the most important, to the pilot at least, was that for operating the canopy. The primary control was the crank lever, which moved the canopy back and forth. Also included within these cranks, ratchets, and levers was an external control that allowed the canopy to be locked closed from the outside by a spring-loaded locking bolt. Another mechanically operated mechanism was the footstep, located on the port side of the fuselage just aft of the wing. Although it was connected to a lever in the cockpit, a final check was required before departure, as a slightly open step

Sea Fury FB.11 TF 963 is up on jacks and trestles. (W A Harrison Collection)

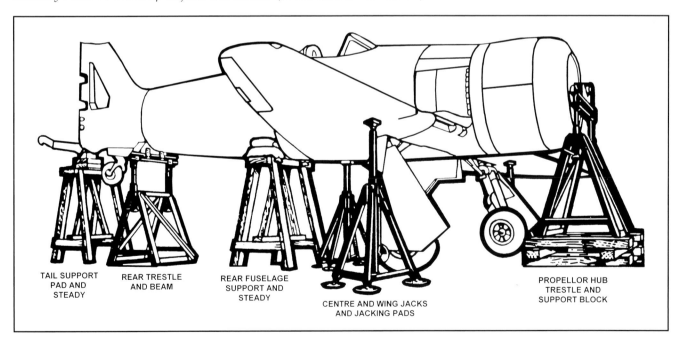

TAIL SUPPORT PAD AND STEADY

REAR TRESTLE AND BEAM

REAR FUSELAGE SUPPORT AND STEADY

CENTRE AND WING JACKS AND JACKING PADS

PROPELLOR HUB TRESTLE AND SUPPORT BLOCK

When the Sea Fury required maintenance, it could be raised off the ground using jacks and supported by trestles. The forward trestle was very rarely used, as a weight was the preferred method of counterbalancing. (Based on material supplied by the FAAM)

This is a view of the starboard undercarriage bay and the main gear mechanism. The open flap in front of the bay is used to dump excess cooling air. (Big Bird Aviation Collection)

cover would allow exhaust fumes to be drawn into the cockpit. The second footstep in the side of the fuselage closed automatically when the gear retracted.

A final footstep was located in the wing root, although this one sprung shut once the foot was removed.

From a three-quarter angle, the assembly of the main gear leg and its suspension link can be seen clearly. (Big Bird Aviation Collection)

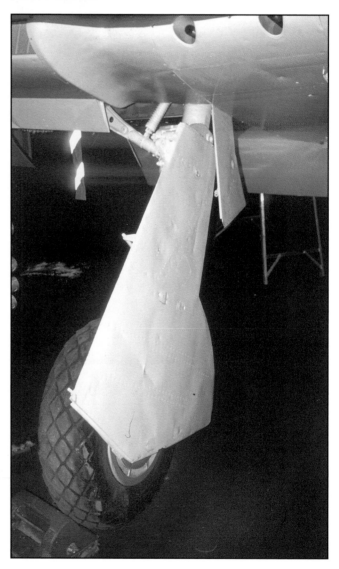

On each main leg, the primary fairing is fixed, and only the small upper panel has a need to move. (Big Bird Aviation Collection)

An extensive lighting system inside the cockpit illuminated the gauges and controls. Three kinds of lights were installed in the Sea Fury—the dimmable ultraviolet lamps, the controllable red lamps, and an emergency setup that consisted of a single lamp, complete with its own battery. Other lights were spread around the external points of the airframe. These were divided into three distinct categories. The first were the

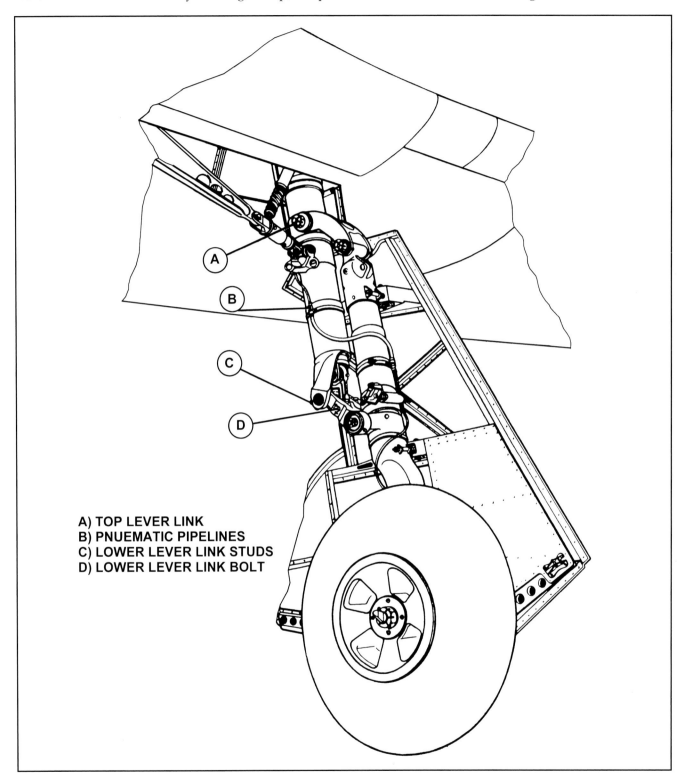

A) TOP LEVER LINK
B) PNUEMATIC PIPELINES
C) LOWER LEVER LINK STUDS
D) LOWER LEVER LINK BOLT

The Sea Fury leg consisted of an upper mounting tube to which a separate shock absorber was connected via swinging links. (Based on material supplied by the FAAM)

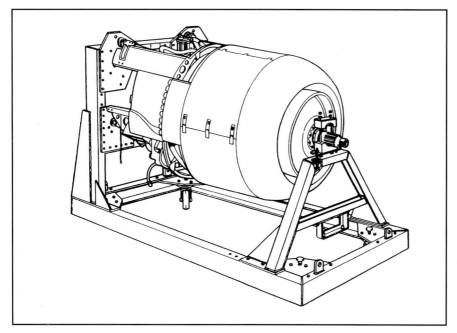

The Centaurus engine was normally delivered on a special to type transit stand. (Based on material supplied by the FAAM)

identification lights under the starboard wing, which were red and green, while that under the other wing was amber. Four navigation lights were located at the wingtips and on each side of the tail unit. Interconnected with these lamps was the arrestor hook, whose activation would operate the lights to help the carrier deck batsman see the aircraft under any conditions. The third external lighting system included the attitude lights, located on the port main gear leg and the port tailwheel door. Mainly intended for night, they were intended to help the deck landing batsman during night operations.

Although the pilot's cockpit was festooned with controls and lights, one of the most important mechanisms was the oxygen system. The cylinders that provided this vital breathing gas were held in cradles under the cockpit floor. Control was via a regulator on the right-hand side of the pilot's panel. Other equipment associated with the pilot's environment were the heater for the pressure head and windscreen deicing. Further controllable elements for the pilot's safety and comfort included air conditioning, which could be controlled by the use of a hand wheel that moved between cold and warm, although cold air was only available for the upper part of the cockpit canopy. A de-icing system was designed to help the pilot to see in the most adverse conditions. This was a fluid-based system that had a tank in the port wheel bay and was jetted up to the screen by a separate pump. The final and possibly most important item within the cockpit

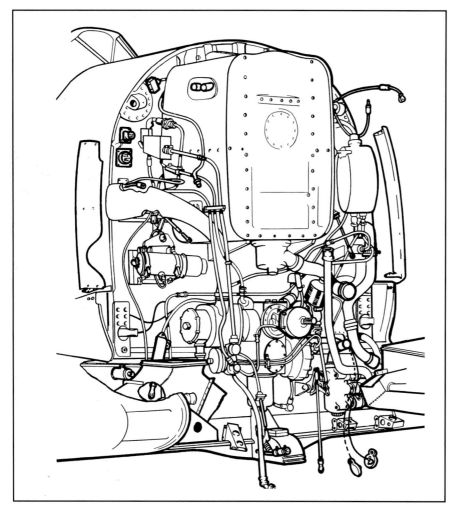

In contrast to the jet engine, a piston engine could be a very complicated beast to install as this view of the firewall reveals. (Based on material supplied by the FAAM)

was, of course, the pilot's seat and combined head rest. This could be adjusted by the use of a lever on the right-hand side. A release lever in the cockpit allowed the pilot to move without disconnecting from the safety harness, but, unfortunately, the headrest was fitted to the armor-plated seat and was not movable.

Beyond the items needed to control and operate the Sea Fury, a look is needed at the systems furnished so the aircraft could fulfill its operational role. The first of these are the weapons controls, most of which were under the guidance of the Mk. 4B gyro gunsight. Not only did this unit have a reticule adjustable for guns and rockets, it also came equipped with a camera recorder and a source of illumination. The four 20mm Hispano cannons were fired electrically using a switch on the spade grip, which could also be used for bomb release, rocket firing,

The short-barreled Hispano cannons were flush with the wing's leading edge. Note the dished recesses. Close observation of the wing under skin shows the forward mount for the underwing fuel tank. (Big Bird Aviation Collection)

and the cine camera. For safety, a cut-out switch coupled to the undercarriage locks prevented the guns from firing accidentally upon the ground. For ground use, a butt test switch was fitted in the starboard

This particular Sea Fury is parked with its wings folded and flaps down. Close observation of the wing break point shows the piping for the wing fold and locking pin system. (Big Bird Aviation Collection)

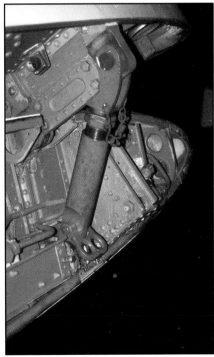

To stop the wing from inadvertently moving, a lock such as this is fitted. (Big Bird Aviation Collection)

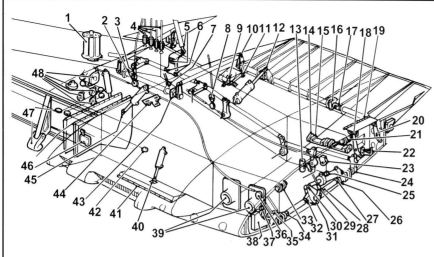

The wing center section contained many of the hydraulic components and most of the flying controls passed through this zone. (Based on material supplied by the FAAM)

center wing section to allow the weapons to fire at gun butts, when requiring harmonization. The cine camera was mounted in the port wing and had a selector that allowed adjustment for sunny or cloudy weather. One little known role of the Sea Fury was that of photo reconnaissance. To carry out this task, provisions were made for the installation of both vertical and oblique cameras whose control box could be mounted in the cockpit.

Further systems which could be installed on the Sea Fury include the RATOG equipment, and two buttons were associated with this sys-

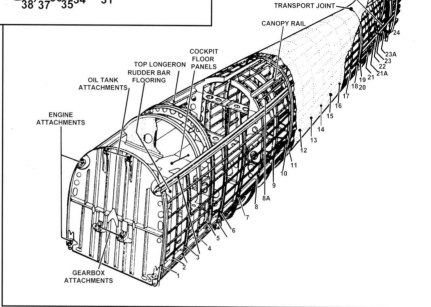

The fuselage was built in three sections, connected by numerous nuts and bolts. (Based on material supplied by the FAAM)

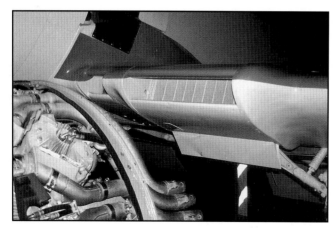

This general view of the port wing shows the leading edge cooling intake, the recessed cannon mounts, and the main gear assembly. (Big Bird Aviation Collection)

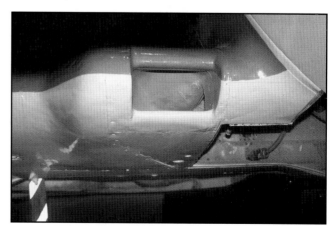

This is the cooling radiator, located at the junction between the fuselage and the starboard wing. (Big Bird Aviation Collection)

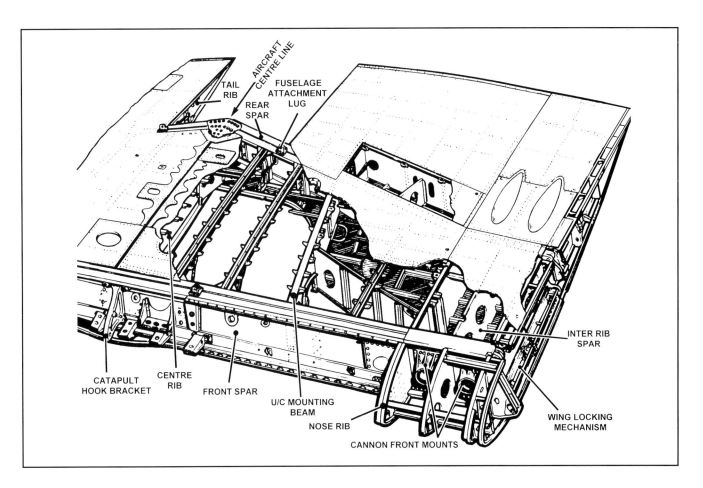

TAIL RIB
AIRCRAFT CENTRE LINE
FUSELAGE ATTACHMENT LUG
REAR SPAR
INTER RIB SPAR
CATAPULT HOOK BRACKET
CENTRE RIB
FRONT SPAR
U/C MOUNTING BEAM
NOSE RIB
WING LOCKING MECHANISM
CANNON FRONT MOUNTS

The center section (above) of the Sea Fury was the strongest component in the airframe, as many of the crash photos show. The outer wing panels (below) were built around two main spars and one sub spar, to which the ribs and stringers were attached. (Based on material supplied by the FAAM)

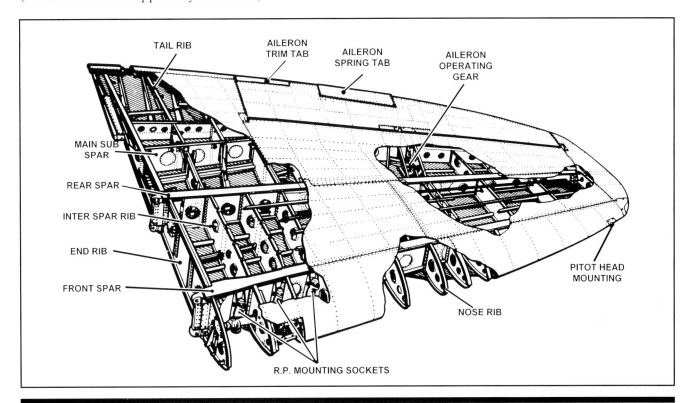

TAIL RIB
AILERON TRIM TAB
AILERON SPRING TAB
AILERON OPERATING GEAR
MAIN SUB SPAR
REAR SPAR
INTER SPAR RIB
END RIB
FRONT SPAR
PITOT HEAD MOUNTING
NOSE RIB
R.P. MOUNTING SOCKETS

tem. One covered the ignition, while the other would jettison the rockets when they were spent. The Sea Fury was protected from missile attack by 'windows' deception chaff. The controller had four launch positions, excluding the off position, which regulated the dispensing of this radar deceiver. Other ancillary equipment included the flare launcher and the wing camera container.

For an aircraft of this era, the Sea Fury was remarkably well equipped with avionics. The radio system was based on the ARI 5491 VHF airborne relay unit, plus a standard four-channel VHF transmitter-receiver. When radar was installed in the Sea Fury, the preferred system was the ARI 5307 ZBX installation, which could be integrated with the VHF relay unit. Other avionics equipment, involved mainly with navigation, included the altimeter and the G4F compass.

Above and Below: *This dismantled Sea Fury T.Mk. 20 reveals much of the detail surrounding the wing center section and engine bulkhead.* (Mark Russell)

Although the Hawker Sea Fury can be regarded as the last fling of the piston era, it was remarkable how well equipped it was, and how much of its equipment would appear in the jet aircraft that would follow.

HANDLING 4 THE BEAST

Although the Hawker Sea Fury was one of the fastest seagoing piston-powered fighters ever built, it could be a real handful, especially for the tyro pilot. The Fleet Air Arm and Hawker Aircraft eventually came up with the Sea Fury T.20 for the training role, but there were still accidents.

Pilots who climbed into the cockpit of the Sea Fury had a whole raft of instructions and mnemonics to learn. Once these were ingrained into the airman's consciousness, operation of the big fighter became easier.

One of the first areas in which new pilots are thoroughly trained is managing the fuel system. The most important item needing consideration was that of managing the drop tanks. When the wing external tanks were not fitted, the selector lever had to be in the off position, or the internal tanks would be isolated and the contents gauges would read incorrectly. In contrast, when they were fitted, both selector valves had to be in the on position. The tanks had to be isolated once they were drained to stop any chance of main system feed back.

With the fuel system covered, the instructor would normally move onto the complexities of engine starting and handling. The first item on the agenda covered the prestart procedure (see insert).

Another prestart check required that the propeller be turned through two complete revolutions by hand to reduce the possibility of hydraulic shock damage, caused by pressurised fuel trapped in the engine at ignition. With the foregoing successfully completed, the fuel injector button would then be depressed for 30 seconds to prime the system. A further amount of button pushing was sometimes required if the high pressure priming modification, N.22, had been incorporated. This action was required for only five seconds, although this was extended

SEA FURY PRESTART PROCEDURE

1.	Ignition switches	OFF
2.	Main fuel cock	ON
3.	Booster pump	OFF
4.	Fuel cut-off control	CUT OFF
5.	Throttle	50 % OPEN
6.	RPM control lever	MAXIMUM
7.	Air intake heat control	OFF
8.	Air intake filter control	CLEAN or FILTER
9.	Engine cooling shutters	OPEN
10.	Supercharger control	M (low gear)
11.	Depress the booster pump circuit	(if required)

Not an unusual occurrence for a Sea Fury, although it does allow all the upper surface detail to be seen. (W A Harrison Collection)

This Sea Fury FB.11 TF898 is parked with its flaps in the "max" position. (W A Harrison Collection)

to at least 15 seconds on premodification engines. Once the priming was satisfactory, the ignition was moved to the "on" position and the button depressed. If the priming was right, the Centaurus should turn over and run smoothly. As it could be cantankerous at times, it was recommended that the priming button be pushed until the engine was running sweetly. However, should none of the foregoing work,

there were further instructions. Sometimes a cartridge in the Coffman starter breech would not exert enough force to turn the engine over. Counteracting this required selection of another cartridge and its immediate ignition, plus depression of the combined starter and booster coil button. If this failed to work, the sequence had to be abandoned for 30 seconds. Consequently, should further tries be required beyond

four, the whole sequence had to be abandoned and the engine turned over to the engineers for investigation. After a successful start however, the powerplant needed to be run at a constant 1,200 rpm to allow for a thorough warmup.

Even though the engine was by then running, further checks were required to ensure its consistency in-flight, these mainly involving the cylinder head temperatures and magnetos. With all complete, the throttle needed to be opened to check the output of the mounted generator. Even this had extra precautions, which involved pulling the control column fully back to stop the Sea Fury from tipping over on its nose, a favorite trick of the type. With everything running correctly, the propeller needs functioning throughout its gearing range, and final checks must be made on the magnetos. Once completed, the Sea Fury can depart for takeoff.

While operating from an airfield, the Sea Fury required the use of full throttle during takeoff. One interesting proviso that needed observation was the requirement for full throttle to be maintained, even if the aircraft lifted off before the final position was reached. As with all piston-powered airframes, the Sea Fury required rudder control to maintain its direction, although taking off with the tail held in the down position made the whole process much easier. This was a definite requirement when the flaps were in the takeoff or max lift position. Once the Sea Fury was airborne, the brakes had to be applied prior to retraction to stop the wheels spinning in the main gear bays. One foible of the Hawker design was that on odd occasions the undercarriage lights would show red, indicating an

The amount of damage that could be inflicted upon the Sea Fury was tremendous. The pilot walked away from this total wreck. (W A Harrison Collection)

unlocked status. The advice given in such circumstances was to throttle back to reduce forward airspeed, which normally allowed the legs to complete their upward travel.

In contrast to the ground takeoff, the carrier departure required the use of the flaps at the takeoff setting with the elevators trimmed slightly nose-up. The throttle had to be set to maximum against the brakes in order to give the pilot some leeway on power during catapult launch, and the tail had to be held down for as long as possible. The final check prior to launch was to ensure that the tail wheel was locked to stop castoring, while the rudder needed to be held in the central position to stop the aircraft crabbing.

The Sea Fury had the capability to mount the RATOG system to assist it off the ground when fully laden, although there were strict regulations governing its use. The first point for the pilot was to define the exact firing point on the runway to ignite the rockets. Prior to full engine run up, three final requirements had to be observed. The first was to ensure that the flaps were selected to the takeoff position; second, the tail wheel needed to be locked; and third, the RATOG master switch needed to be selected to on. With all checks completed, the Sea Fury was then clear to start its takeoff run, although every effort had to be made to keep the direction of departure as straight as possible. As with all other takeoffs, the tail-down position was the favored option, although in this scenario the control column needed to be offset slightly to port. Once the Sea Fury was fully rolling, the RATOG firing was delayed until the theoretical firing point was reached. At that point, the pilot would depress the button and the ignition

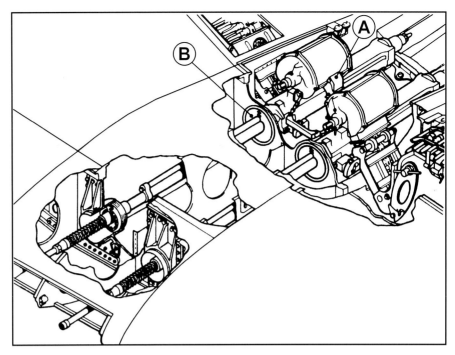

The 20mm Hispano short-barreled cannons were installed in the center section of the wing for stability reasons. (Based on material supplied by the FAAM)

sequence would engage. If at any time there was a misfire or total ignition failure, the takeoff would be aborted as the fighter would be too heavy to proceed.

Given a good ignition, the aircraft

would lift off. The pilot then had to watch carefully for trim changes, the first of which was normally nose up while the rockets continued to fire. Once they had expired, the opposite would happen. All pilots were warned that trying to pull the Sea

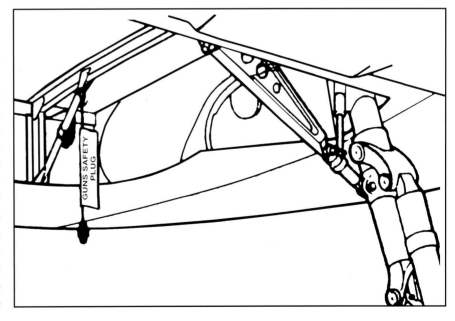

To stop the inadvertent discharge of the Hispano cannons, the undercarriage bay had locations for gun safety pins. (Based on material supplied by the FAAM)

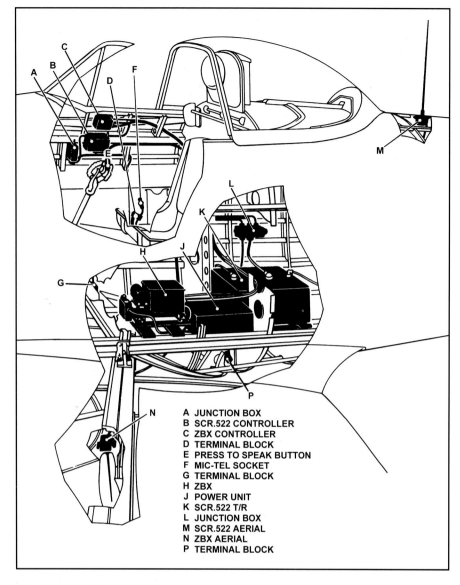

A JUNCTION BOX
B SCR.522 CONTROLLER
C ZBX CONTROLLER
D TERMINAL BLOCK
E PRESS TO SPEAK BUTTON
F MIC-TEL SOCKET
G TERMINAL BLOCK
H ZBX
J POWER UNIT
K SCR.522 T/R
L JUNCTION BOX
M SCR.522 AERIAL
N ZBX AERIAL
P TERMINAL BLOCK

The Sea Fury was well equipped with avionics systems, even though it was designed in the late 1940s. (Based on material supplied by the FAAM)

Fury off the ground early would result in a stall, and a serious starboard wing drop would occur. Once clear of the ship or the ground, the flaps needed to be raised quickly so that a level speed of 150 knots could readily be achieved. Once this point had been reached, the RATOG carriers could be ejected and the switch turned to off. The sudden change of weight and balance always induced a nose-down trim change.

Once airborne, the Sea Fury could be climbed initially at a speed of 165 knots from sea level to 20,000 feet, after which it would be acceptable to let the speed drop off by five knots per every 4,000 feet. A further instruction to the pilot does however contradict this, as it states that the optimum speed for climbing to height is a steady 185 knots.

The Sea Fury's behavior in the air has always been described as pleasant to fly at all heights and speeds, although the aircraft has a tendency to tighten in the turn at high altitudes. Trim changes were marginal, although nose-down could be induced by extending the undercarriage, lowering the flaps, and fully opening the engine cooling shutters. In the opposite direction, retracting the undercarriage, moving the flaps to the closed position, and closing the engine shutters would cause the nose to rise. A final proviso mentioned that under no circumstances should the engine cooling flaps be operated in a dive.

Other handling points to consider covered stalling speeds at various weights and speeds. With gear

From the extent of the damage, it would appear that this aircraft had ground looped severely on touchdown, the cause possibly being heavy braking. (W A Harrison Collection)

retracted and flaps up, the stalling speed of the aircraft at 12,400 lb. was 105 knots, although this increased to 115 knots at the greater weight of 14,650 lb. Further changes occurred with the gear and flaps down, when at the lower weight the stalling speed was reduced to 90 knots, while at the higher weight it increased to 100 knots. In the normal power-on approach pattern, the stalling speed reduced even further to 80 knots. Warning of a stall was first revealed by the tail unit dropping, after which the nose would drop. Trying to correct this by pulling the control column back would result in the ailerons snatching, followed by the nose and port wing dropping. Obviously extreme care needed to be taken on approaching to land, as a stall unchecked could result in a crash. Under these conditions the first warnings were revealed by aileron snatching and a change in nose attitude upward. Counteracting this required a large amount of left rudder to maintain direction. If it was allowed to develop, the stall caused the starboard wing to drop sharply, since this was the direction of the torque generated by the engine. Recovery required closing the throttle and centralizing the controls.

Spinning an aircraft unintentionally is one of a pilot's greatest dreads. Some aircraft have excellent recovery behavior while others are lethal in the extreme. Intentional spinning in the Sea Fury was banned although if it should happen by accident, normal recovery action was recommended. Pulling out of the resultant dive, however, had to wait until a speed of 175 knots had been reached. As a fighter bomber, the Sea Fury was expected to dive on targets occasionally and was very stable in such an attitude, although care had to be

This fine airborne shot is of FB.11 VX639 of the second line unit No. 738 Squadron. Its only external load appears to be underwing rocket rails. (W A Harrison Collection)

taken not to exceed the limiting top speed which could result in airframe overstress. There was a noted slight tendency to yaw in the dive, which needed correcting by use of the trim tab, and care was needed at such high speeds as the controls became extremely sensitive. In view of the

behavior of the Sea Fury under various flight conditions, it might be surprising to learn that it was a very aerobatic aircraft, although there were limits to flying speeds which ranged from 200 to 400 knots.

Having covered many of the aspects

The result of bad landing is evidenced by FB.11 WG599, standing on its nose aboard HMS Warrior *in 1954. The Sea Fury has lost a fuel tank sometime during the incident, but still has both bomb shackles mounted. (W A Harrison Collection)*

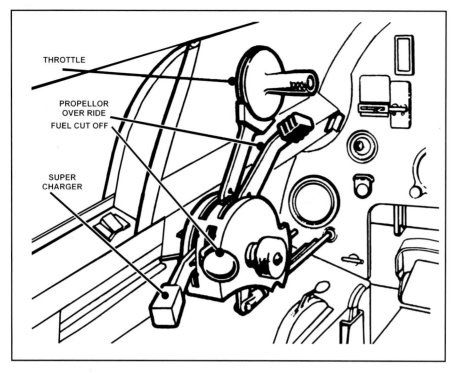

THROTTLE

PROPELLOR
OVER RIDE
FUEL CUT OFF

SUPER
CHARGER

Control of the engine was via these four levers. One controlled the fuel feed, another the supercharger, another the propeller override, and the last was the throttle itself. (Based on material supplied by the FAAM)

of flying the Sea Fury the most important and difficult phase needs to be considered. This is the approach and landing sequence, which many pilots reckon to be the most difficult aspect of aircraft handling. From this point of view, the Sea Fury was no different from other aircraft, as it too would behave quite properly as long as the limits were observed. Defined limits for a typical service load encompassing an all up weight of 12,400 lb. meant that a speed of 100 knots had to be observed when both the flaps and undercarriage were extended. This increased to 115 knots when the flaps were retracted. Separate limits were in force when the aircraft was operating at its maximum landing weight of 14,000 lb. These were nominally 10 knots above the lighter weight. In both circumstances the initial approach speed was recommended to be some 10 to 15 knots higher.

In contrast, the engine-off performance called for a different set of operating parameters, the primary item of which was that any landing should see the undercarriage extended and the flaps in the takeoff position. Careful handling meant that a steady speed of 130 knots could be maintained throughout the approach. As soon as the destination airfield was in sight, the flaps were to be selected to max lift. The final round out and approach should be carried out at 130 knots before the Sea Fury was slowed down to 115 knots over the boundary. Any attempt to execute a landing with the flaps in the fully down position would result in a very steep glide path and a heavy landing that could cause overstress of the airframe.

Deck landing on an aircraft carrier under similar conditions required that a similar speed be maintained, although the extra drag of the lowered arrestor hook needed to be taken into account and the tail wheel needed to be in the unlocked position. Unlike landing on an airfield, the round out speed required for an aircraft carrier was only 90 knots, although the control column needed to be fully back to achieve a three-point landing.

Like all pilots, the Hawker Sea Fury pilot was trained to deal with various emergencies, the first of which was undercarriage malfunction. Whatever the circumstances, either

FB.11 VW582 sits on the ground with its wings folded and tailwheel in the unlocked position. (W A Harrison Collection)

the legs failing to lower or the lights not running through their sequence, the first action was to select the back-up system. The operation required stamina on behalf of the pilot, as the flaps needed to be pumped down by hand to the max lift setting, should the engine pump have failed. This hard work entailed some 80 double strokes for full extension, especially if the undercarriage lights were indicating that the legs are unlocked. Once the flaps were down, the Sea Fury was then slowed to 115 knots.

Further hand pumping would then be required to get the undercarriage down and locked and to get the lights to go green. This could entail a further 120 double strokes, although the proviso in this operation stated that if the gear did not unlock in the first 12 strokes, that other measures would be needed. These entailed the use of the emergency lowering system, the first pull of which should cause the locks to withdraw and the legs to move downward as gravity took effect. A second pull of the same handle released a pneumatic

With flaps set at takeoff, this Sea Fury departs its carrier, courtesy of its RATOG units. (Fleet Air Arm Museum)

charge that would blow the gear down and locked. However, should even this operation not complete successfully, it was recommended that the pilot maintain a speed of 115 knots and use the rudder to induce yawing. The drop of the nose normally induced the gear to finally lock, although if all else has failed, it was recommended that the pilot bail out. If, on the other hand, the gear came down and locked and all the

lights went green, the pilot was to check the visual pins to confirm the status. Only the main gear legs required assistance to extend, as hydraulic failure causes the tail leg to lower.

On later build aircraft, Mod N.30 removed the need for the hand pump, as the emergency blow-down system was utilized from the outset. As the gear was the most needed

Taxiing out to start a training sortie, this FB.11 sports rocket rails under the wings. (C P Russell Smith Collection)

system, it was lowered first with the flaps following soon after. As the undercarriage would utilize most of the available pneumatic pressure, the flaps would only move to their final position when power and speed were lowered for the final approach.

Not only could the undercarriage give problems, but the flap hydraulic system could also fail. However, flapless landings were not quite the problem that the lack of undercarriage could cause, as a normal length runway could be successfully negotiated even in a light wind. The approach under such circumstances had to be flown as flat as possible and large throttle movements were to be avoided. A typical service load of 12,400 lb. gave an approach speed of 120 knots, which reduces by 10 knots at the threshold. At that point, the throttle was cut and a three-point landing effected.

This Sea Fury FB.11 VX653 has recently undergone a major servicing, as the painted exhaust panel shows. A few flights, and the paint will be burned off. (W A Harrison Collection)

Loss of engine power also gave cause for concern and could be caused in many ways. One of the most common was sustained negative Gs or inverted flight, which could cause the fuel system to cut out. To counteract this, the Sea Fury needed to be turned the right way up and the throttle and the fuel cut off levers had to be shut. After a short period of some 10 seconds, recovery could begin. This centered about repriming the injectors and restoring power. Any other form of power failure associated with engine malfunctioning either led to the loss

Sometimes an uncontrolled landing onboard a carrier went wrong, as in this case, in which the Sea Fury has jumped the barrier. (Fleet Air Arm Museum)

of the aircraft or the pilot having to make a dead stick landing at the nearest airfield.

Should any situation become unrecoverable, the pilot was also briefed on abandoning a stricken Sea Fury. The first step to escaping required the jettisoning of the canopy and the cockpit side entrance panel. To ensure that the canopy cleared the airframe properly, a minimum speed of 210 knots was required. On Sea Furies that were not modified to Mod.339 standard, it was recommended that the canopy be opened at least an inch to help the latches disengage properly. On the post-modification aircraft, this extra effort was not required. There was an external jettison handle under a perspex glass cover near the port wing fillet to help rescuers gain access to a Sea Fury pilot after a crash landing.

In the event that the Sea Fury had to be ditched, the pilot cleared the canopy as described earlier before clearing the underwing of any stores or tanks, which allowed the aircraft to ditch correctly. Within this time frame, hopefully the pilot would be able to send out a radio distress message before disconnecting from the aircraft radio connecting plug. The next step, which was possible with the engine running, was to lower the flaps fully and pull the control column back to lower the tail, so that the slowest possible landing speed could be achieved. In contrast, engine failure reduced the flap droop available to 30 degrees.

Having overshot the arrestor wires, this Sea Fury is about to impact the barrier erected for just such an occasion. (Fleet Air Arm Museum)

The arrestor hook fitted to the Sea Fury was a substantial affair. (Big Bird Aviation Collection)

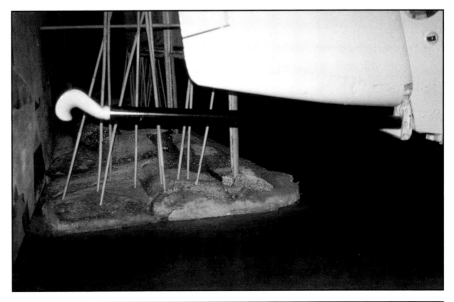

This brand new Sea Fury FB.11 is being boarded by its pilot, after having been on display at the SBAC show at Radlett in 1949. (C P Russell Smith Collection)

Any more would increase the sink rate to an unacceptable level and cause possible misjudgment of the touchdown. A further instruction states that the Sea Fury was to be landed along the swell or into the wind, with the pilot abandoning the aircraft via the port side.

Over land a similar series of actions needed to be observed, the first being to issue a distress signal via the radio. This was then followed by the requirement to clear the complete underwing stores complement and to jettison the canopy and side panel. Prior to touchdown the seat harness was to be tightened and locked. Once the touchdown site was selected, the flaps needed to be lowered to the takeoff setting and speed should be controlled at 130 knots. On approach, the flaps should be dropped to max lift prior to controlling the touchdown. One of the main reasons for making a crash or belly landing was, surprisingly, that of a tire burst. The Sea Fury with a burst tire was known to have a tendency to either tip on its nose or flip over completely. Under these conditions, the damage caused by touching down with the gear up was deemed the lesser of two evils.

Departing from RNAS Ford is this Sea Fury FB.11, which has only bomb carriers under the wings. (C P Russell Smith Collection)

Instructions were issued to the pilot on how to abandon the Sea Fury, should the need arise. However these did not take into account the possibility of having to escape under combat conditions. Many of the instructions were the same as those for crash landing or ditching, although a nose-down attitude required the use of the elevator trim.

With its flaps and hook deployed, this Sea Fury is caught just prior to touchdown. Note the open canopy, required should there be an emergency. (Fleet Air Arm Museum)

THE SEA FURY IN KOREA

With the deliveries of the Hawker Sea Fury progressing steadily to the front line squadrons, they were split into three carrier air groups and assigned to distinct vessels. The First Carrier Air Group, assigned to the fleet carrier HMS *Ocean*, consisted of No. 802 Squadron, equipped with the Hawker Sea Fury FB.11, and No. 825 Squadron, operating the multi-role Fairey Firefly Mk. 5. Embarked on HMS *Theseus* was the Seventeenth Carrier Air Group, whose No.

807 Squadron was flying the Sea Fury and No. 810 Squadron the Firefly. The final CAG, the Fourteenth, was assigned to HMS *Glory*, with No. 804 Squadron operating the Hawker fighter while No. 812 Squadron flew the Firefly.

On 25 June 1950 the forces of North Korea began their invasion of the southern territories below the 38th parallel. In response, the United Nations assembled a multinational task force to assist the beleaguered

South Korean forces in their repulsion of the northern invaders. The seagoing part of the British response, as designated by the Admiralty, drew initially on the ships of the Far East Fleet. From its base in Hong Kong, the light fleet carrier HMS *Triumph*, with No. 800 Squadron, equipped with Supermarine Seafire FR.47s, and No. 827 Squadron, flying Fireflies, was dispatched to Korean territorial waters, arriving on 30 June. In concert with its support group of two cruisers,

With engines running, the Sea Furies of HMS Theseus *prepare to depart on another sortie. Although most of the aircraft have rocket rails, these are not loaded as the fighters are scheduled for CAP sorties.* (Fleet Air Arm Museum)

Launching from the carrier, this Sea Fury FB.11 has an underwing load of fuel tanks and 250-lb conventional bombs. (Fleet Air Arm Museum)

two destroyers, and three frigates, the airwing of the *Triumph* CAG began its operations on 3 July in conjunction with the Vought F-4U Corsairs and Douglas Skyraiders from the aircraft carrier USS *Valley Forge*. These were the first naval air strikes of the war. HMS *Triumph* remained on station for the follow-

ing three months, during which a total of 895 sorties were flown.

As the tour of duty for HMS *Triumph* was coming to a close, its replacement, HMS *Theseus*, was warned for dispatch, in company with its support group, from United Kingdom waters. Departing in late August

1950, the fleet carrier collected its aircraft that made up the Seventeenth CAG on the way, when they flew from their home base of RNAS Lee on Solent. An intensive period of operational work up flying occupied both the Sea Furies and Fireflies over the following six weeks, as the carrier crossed the seas between the UK and the Far East. This was necessary to integrate the new pilots recently posted into the squadron. Although most of the pilots of No. 807 Squadron were experienced in carrier operations, there was the usual spate of landing accidents, some attributable to excessive braking. These sudden stops frequently resulted in the Sea Fury tipping up on its nose, and some flipped over completely. The decision on damage repair depended on the resources. If the airframe was repairable, it was taken below. Otherwise, a full spares recovery program was carried out, and the remains were dumped over the side of the ship.

Upon *Theseus'* arrival in the Far East, the fleet aviation officer made contact with the Tactical Air Control Center, only to discover that the center was totally unaware of the arrival of the aircraft carrier and its capabilities.

HMS *Theseus* arrived on station in Korean waters on 9 October, allowing HMS *Triumph* to depart. Immediately on HMS *Theseus'* arrival in the Yellow Sea, the Seventeenth CAG began flying operations. These continued until 22 October, with targets at Chinnampo, Heiju in Hwanghai Province, Pakchong, and Chongju being attacked. Many of these strikes were directed at Chinnampo, as the United Nations land forces had aspirations to capture it from the North Koreans and use it as a supply port and jumping off point for further operations.

Even in the depths of winter, operations continued. The carrier deck is snow covered, and more bad weather apparently is expected, as the Sea Fury in the foreground (right) has a rudder clamp fitted to protect the airframe. (Fleet Air Arm Museum)

During this period of intensive flying, the Hawker Sea Furies of No. 807 Squadron achieved a total of 264 combat sorties, while the Firefly unit, No. 810, managed to notch up 120 missions. After this short period on station, HMS *Theseus* was withdrawn for a period of rest, replenishment, and recuperation at the Japanese port of Iwakuni. Also located here were a cadre of replacement aircraft and maintenance engineers whose task it was to keep the flying inventory up to operational strength. While in port, it was discovered that the running mechanism for the catapult had become excessively worn. This required that aircraft requiring launch needed RATOG assistance. As this needed a longer deck run, it was decided that six of the Fireflies would remain in Japan to increase the available deck space.

Combat operations were resumed on 27 October and were to last until 5 November 1950, with HMS *Theseus* providing cover for minesweeping operations in the Chinnampo estuary. This return to combat was cut short, as HMS *Theseus* returned to Hong Kong to take part in a combined services exercise. During this period the Seventeenth CAG was running light, as the remaining Fireflies of No. 810 Squadron remained in Korea to provide aircraft for artillery spotting duties. The carrier returned to resume operations under the command of Vice Admiral Andrews in the Yellow Sea on 7 December, these lasting until 15 December. During this period the targets that the air wing concentrated on included roads, bridges, airfields, and railway rolling stock. Secondary targets were strategic or transport in nature, with the aim of disrupting the North Korean logistics chain and slowing the arrival of Chinese troops as much as possible. During this period some

Turning over the Korean countryside, this FB.11 is carry external tanks only for its patrol duties. (Fleet Air Arm Museum)

332 sorties were flown without loss, although the ship's helicopter was attacked by MiG fighters while rescuing personnel from the Chanyan area. Fortunately, a replacement flight of Sea Furies arrived on the scene and drove the attackers away, saving the helicopter.

Aboard the crowded deck of HMS Ocean, *a vast profusion of Sea Furies is assembled. During most operations, the catapult was the preferred method of launch, as RATOG was slower in execution.* (Fleet Air Arm Museum)

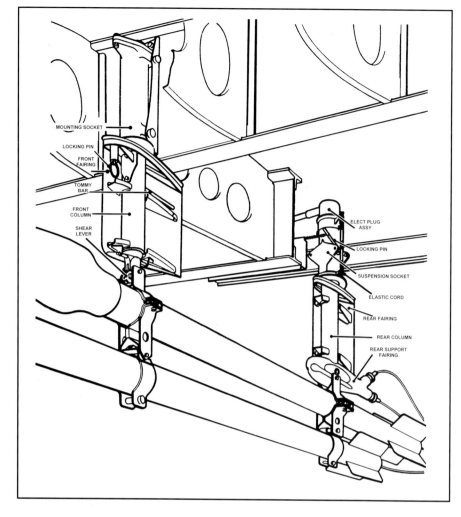

MOUNTING SOCKET
LOCKING PIN
FRONT FAIRING
TOMMY BAR
FRONT COLUMN
SHEAR LEVER

ELECT PLUG ASSY
LOCKING PIN
SUSPENSION SOCKET
ELASTIC CORD
REAR FAIRING
REAR COLUMN
REAR SUPPORT FAIRING

The Sea Fury was capable of carrying three double banks of rocket projectiles, although experience in Korea reduced this to just one. (Based on material supplied by the FAAM)

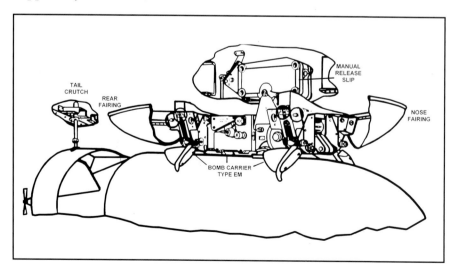

TAIL CRUTCH
REAR FAIRING
MANUAL RELEASE SLIP
NOSE FAIRING
BOMB CARRIER TYPE EM

The faired bomb mounting was locked on to the wing using one mounting point, which was capable of manual release in an emergency. (Based on material supplied by the FAAM)

Throughout this period, the aircraft of the Seventeenth CAG encountered very little in the way of airborne resistance, the greater source of damage being from the intensive antiaircraft fire put up by the North Koreans, or by technical problems. At least one pilot from No. 807 Squadron, Lieutenant D. P. W. Kelly, was to experience the latter source the hard way. On 24 December 1950, shortly after departing the carrier, the Centaurus engine began to malfunction and finally quit altogether. Although full water tank tests had been carried out to determine the behavior of the Sea Fury in the sea, many pilots were distrustful of this information. However, the pilot followed instructions, cleared the underwing of stores and successfully ditched into the sea, some four miles in front of HMS *Theseus*. He was quickly recovered by a U.S. Navy destroyer, USS *Sioux*, and returned to HMS *Theseus*, resuming flying duties the next day. The number of sorties flown over this period eventually reached 630 in total. In recognition of its activities during 1950, the Seventeenth CAG was awarded the Boyd Trophy, which is awarded to the airman, unit, ship, or station that has made the greatest contribution to naval aviation during the year.

Other duties covered by the aircraft of the Seventeenth CAG included combat air patrols and antisubmarine patrols in search of the two vessels reportedly being operated by the North Korean Navy. In this latter role the Fireflies were operated with external long-range fuel tanks. While engaged on CAP duties, the Sea Furies managed 3,900 interceptions, all of which were allied aircraft of one sort or another. In contrast, many of the later missions assigned to the Sea Furies from HMS *Theseus* con-

cerned the provision of top fighter cover for inbound strike forces. These flights occupied the squadron until early 1951, when the mission parameters changed to artillery spotting for Allied naval forces engaged in the bombardment of targets in and around Inchon before moving onto Wonsan and Songiin. As well as the naval support role, the Sea Furies racked up nearly 3,500 sorties during which it dropped 92 of the 1,000-lb. bombs plus 1,400 of the lighter 500-lb. bombs. During the lower level sorties, the fighters expended some 7,300 rocket projectiles and fired over 500,000 rounds of 20mm ammunition. Given the local area, it is not surprising that the weather during the winter months bordered upon the atrocious. Even so, the aircraft of the Seventeenth CAG continued their sortie rate. However, losses accounted for 14 aircraft and six pilots. A further four pilots were rescued by planeguard Sikorsky S-51 helicopters, whose pilots also undertook daring rescues behind enemy lines to secure the safety of another four.

During the period that HMS *Theseus* was on station in the Yellow Sea, the normal complement of Sea Furies assigned to No. 807 Squadron averaged out at 23, although this was subject to combat losses, accidents, and awaiting replacements from Britain. Sortie length for the aircraft of the Seventeenth CAG was a nominal 2-1/2 hours, although this required the use of 45-gallon external tanks to ensure adequate fuel supplies. The Sea Fury was built with RATOG capability, although this was only used on rare occasions. The ship's catapult was the preferred launch medium, although the RATOG system was needed when the Sea Fury was tasked for the bombing role. The reason for this was that HMS *Theseus* had been in

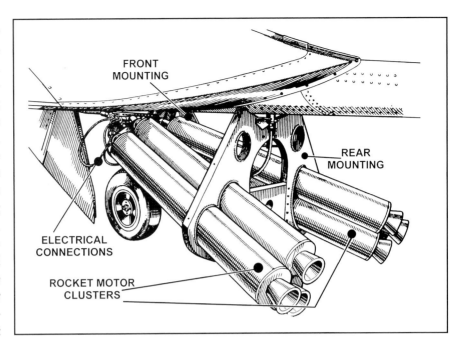

The Sea Fury could be launched by the use of RATOG when there was trouble with the catapult aboard the carrier. After takeoff, the complete installation could be jettisoned. (Based on material supplied by the FAAM)

need of a refit prior to dispatch to the Far East, and the hull was in need of scraping to remove extraneous growths, whose drag through the water was slowing down the ship. This in turn reduced the available top speed to 22 knots, short of the 28 knots required to launch a fully laden Sea Fury. Thus many

missions were tasked as rocket attacks only. Originally the rockets were mounted in multiple racks. However, such was the intensity of operations and the stress of the rocket motors, that the multiple racks and their wing mount points were suffering damage. Eventually the rocket mounts were reduced to sin-

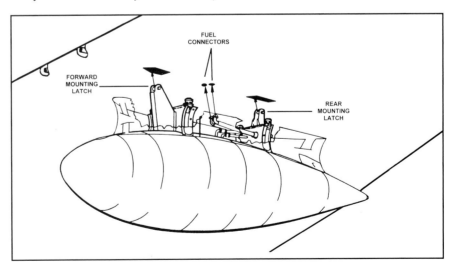

The underwing fuel tanks were mounted with two forks connected into release units, while the fuel was fed through two pipes into the wing. (Based on material supplied by the FAAM)

Running up against its brakes, this FB.11 is connected to the ship's catapult by a single point strop. This aircraft is departing on a ground attack mission, as the rockets under the wings show (W A Harrison Collection)

Sealed against corrosion, this Sea Fury is craned aboard its carrier. Note the missing spinner and main undercarriage doors. (W A Harrison Collection)

gles only. A design fault in the carrier, its inability to store enough ammunition to supply the aircraft, also came to light at this time, but eventually some improvisation overcame this difficulty. Early in the deployment, attempts were made to use the Sea Fury for photo reconnaissance. This was less than successful, as oil ejected from the Centaurus had a tendency to obscure the camera port.

After resuming operations at the beginning of January 1951, the air wing of HMS *Theseus* was hampered in resuming flying sorties due to bad weather. It was not until 12 January that missions were resumed; however, two days later the catapult reeving, which drove the launch, was found to be worn out after completed only 880 launches. To ensure continued flying, the Sea Furies were launched minus their wing tanks and underwing armament, while the Fireflies were dispatched by using the RATOG gear. This allowed them to carry out their missions with a full weapons load, although the covering Sea Furies were armed only with cannons. Even so, both types put in sterling performances in the Suwon-Osan-Inchon area with minimal casualties.

As a port would be required to repair the catapult, the carrier departed to Sasebo for repairs, and was replaced by the USS *Bataan*. Repairs were completed fairly quickly, allowing HMS *Theseus* to return to operations on 25 January. Within six days of returning, the CAG lost four aircraft. Unfortunate-

This Sea Fury from HMS Theseus *is undergoing preparation for a test flight. Note the ground handler stood on the fuselage side footstep.* (C P Russell Smith Collection)

ly one pilot was killed while ditching. Even though the group had suffered losses, it still managed a creditable 66 missions by 3 February. The carrier was withdrawn again as part of the cycle of R&R and combat time. It returned to station in late March, and it was during this period that the self-sealing properties of the fuel tanks in the Sea Fury were found to be ineffective. On 24 March a Sea Fury from the CAG was struck by a half-inch armor-piercing round, which caused extensive damage to the aircraft. Although the aircraft was leaking fuel badly, the pilot managed to achieve an emergency landing at Suwon.

During the following month, reconnaissance and intelligence revealed Communist forces massing near the Yalu River. The response involved intensive operations that lasted from 9 to 15 April and saw strikes carried out against road and rail bridges, rolling stock, marshaling yards, supply dumps, and warehouses. Further missions involved providing aircraft for artillery spotting in the Wonsan and Songjin areas, coupled with armed reconnaissance when needed. During this period, the *Theseus* CAG flew 276 sorties with no deck landing casualties. Five Sea Furies were lost in combat; at least one was shot down by U.S. Marine fighters from Kimpo, and another, VX691, was damaged in the same engagement. With these missions completed, HMS *Theseus* was transferred from the east to the west coast, where it resumed flying operations. During the period 17–18 April, a total of 94 sorties were launched, although at the end of this surge the squadron was running at a reduced complement, having lost further aircraft. After completing this period on station, HMS *Theseus* withdrew to the port at Sasebo for a period of rest

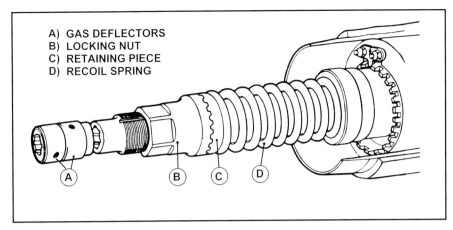

A) GAS DEFLECTORS
B) LOCKING NUT
C) RETAINING PIECE
D) RECOIL SPRING

To counter the recoil of the Hispano cannons when they were fired, large damping springs were installed. (Based on material supplied by the FAAM)

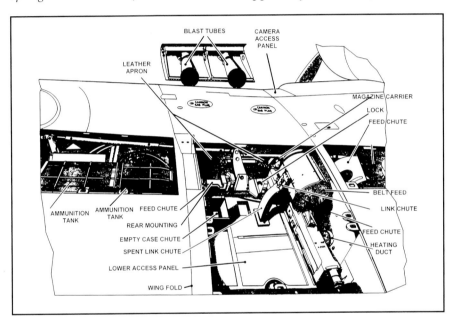

Access to the cannons, ammunition feeds, and tanks was very generous on the Sea Fury, with numerous panels on the upper wing surface. (Based on material supplied by the FAAM)

and recuperation. Statistics on the seven months the carrier had been in combat reveal that during the 86 days of actual flying operations, 3,446 sorties were launched.

On 25 April 1952 HMS *Theseus* was relieved from its second tour of duty on station by HMS *Glory.*

When the fleet carrier HMS *Glory* arrived in the Yellow Sea, it had aboard the aircraft of the Fourteenth

CAG. Its squadrons were No. 804 Squadron, with its complement of Sea Furies increased to 21 aircraft, and No. 812 Squadron, equipped with the Fairey Firefly. Soon after arrival the CAG was engaged in Operation Strangle, a maximum air offensive designed to cut off the North Korean main line of resistance from its logistics tail. The first sortie from HMS *Glory* was launched on 28 April and consisted of 15 aircraft in total, although one Sea Fury was lost

The contemporary to the Sea Fury in the Korean War was the Fairey Firefly, as seen here. (Nick Challoner)

Photographed at RNAS Culdrose, this FB.11 is armed with double racks of 60-lb rocket projectiles. (W A Harrison Collection)

soon after takeoff. Another Sea Fury was lost in a forced landing on 2 May, although in this case the pilot, Lieutenant Barlow, was rescued by the ship's planeguard helicopter. The downed fighter was then strafed and destroyed.

A period of no flying then followed, as the weather was deemed too inhospitable, and it was not until 13 May that flying resumed. Over the next three days a total of 155 missions were launched, during which one Sea Fury was hit by antiaircraft fire, although the pilot was rescued. Four days later, the RN carrier withdrew from Korean waters and was replaced by the USS *Bataan*. However, it was back in the theater by 3 June. Eight days later, a hasty return to port was made to deal with badly contaminated aviation fuel. This had been transferred from RFA *Wave Premier*, whose forward supply pipe work had lain unused for a period, resulting in contamination of the fuel. This was, of course, in total contrast to the tabloid press reports of sabotage. Combat missions began soon after the carrier returned to active duties, although not without cost, as two Sea Furies were lost.

A period in Kure followed before HMS *Glory* resumed combat operations. For once the area was blessed with good weather, which allowed the CAG to dispatch an average of 50 sorties a day. The final two days

Even as the blizzard sweeps across the deck of the HMAS Sydney, crewmembers in their protective clothing are preparing the Sea Furies for another mission. (W A Harrison Collection)

TF956 was originally flown by the Royal Navy Historic Flight before it was lost in a crash. It is captured here on film, as the pilot, Commander John Beattie, desperately attempts to get the stuck undercarriage leg to lower. After following all the instructions in the pilot's manual, the pilot was forced to abandon the aircraft over the sea. (Fleet Air Arm Museum)

saw the carrier using RATOG to launch its aircraft, as the catapult had been damaged during a launch. Even so, the carrier achieved an average of 48 sorties per day, during which a total of 22 1,000-lb. bombs, 200 500-lb. bombs, and 1,500 rockets were dispensed. Within the designated strike zone, all possible trans-

port and communications points were seen as targets and attacked accordingly. The ships within this attack fleet were known as Task Force 95, with the British element being responsible for attacks on the western coast. Such was the intensity of the operations that in one day HMS *Glory* dispatched some 84 com-

bat sorties. Sea Fury losses during this period totaled one, this being the result of a cold shot from the catapult. Four others did have a close call when they were bounced by a flight of four U.S. Air Force P-80s, although no losses were incurred as the piston fighters easily outflew their jet counterparts.

Sea Fury FB.11 WE726 is currently preserved in the Fleet Air Arm Museum in Korean War markings. (W A Harrison Collection)

The primary jet-powered enemy aircraft in Korea was the MiG-15. This is a MiG-15 UTI/Lim2 trainer version. (Nick Challoner)

These Sea Furies are lined up on the deck of HMS Warrior as it enters harbor. The external condition of each airframe is excellent, although this would soon alter after intensive flying. (W A Harrison Collection)

This head-on shot of TF946 reveals the location of the cannons and the camera gun located outboard of the port wing intake. (W A Harrison Collection)

HMS *Glory* resumed combat operations in late July 1951 when the fighting in Korea was at its heaviest. The intensity of the fighting resulted in the loss of two Sea Furies. Other aircraft lost due to engine problems initially were put down to wear and tear. Further investigation revealed that pilots were pushing their aircraft and engines to their limits in order to gain a better edge. The answer was to improve engine maintenance, and thus reliability.

The arrival of Typhoon Madge during the middle of August led to the cancellation of all flying, although a return to operations began again on 1 September. These were hampered again by a malfunctioning catapult, but this did not stop the CAG from averaging 50 sorties per day. The main area of concentration was in and around Han, with Chinnampo and Chongchon also receiving attention, hitting the usual selection of targets. HMS *Glory* was withdrawn from combat operations in October 1951 for rest and recuperation in Singapore. Once this was completed, the carrier departed to Australian waters to carry out its required working up period before returning to station off Korea.

To replace HMS *Glory,* the RAN carrier HMAS *Sydney* moved onto station with Nos. 805 and 808 Squadrons embarked, both operating the Sea Fury. The first mission launched from the Australian carrier took place off the west coast on 5 October, before the ship was transferred to the more target-prolific east. On 11 October HMAS *Sydney* launched 16 Sea Furies to attack targets on the coast and the hills further inland. Roving over the target area, the fighters attacked a force of 2,000 troops digging in. Having located this juicy target, the fighters

attacked, causing numerous casualties and the destruction of an ammunition dump. Three days later, HMAS *Sydney* was withdrawn for a rest, although it resumed operations some four days later. Back on station, the carrier launched its aircraft to attack targets on the coast, including shipping and troop concentrations. During this period three Sea Furies were damaged by antiaircraft fire, causing them to crash land. Fortunately the revised fuel tank protection system had ensured that the fire situation was controlled.

Possibly one of the most daring rescues undertaken during this campaign was the retrieval of Sublieutenant MacWilliams, whose Sea Fury was badly damaged by antiaircraft artillery on 25 October. Although the aircraft was badly damaged, he made a successful crash landing. In an operation reminiscent of later events in Vietnam, the SAR helicopter and five Sea Furies from HMAS *Sydney* were launched to recover the downed airman. Flying top cover was a Meteor F.8 from No. 77 Squadron RAAF. After the Sea Furies fought off the approaching enemy troops, the helicopter rescued the downed pilot. All the aircraft were to reach Kimpo airfield an hour later, just as the light was fading. Further operations were the lot of the Sea Furies from the HMAS *Sydney,* although the winter of 1951 was exceptionally severe, and the weather completely halted flying. On 7 January 1952, HMAS *Sydney* was finally relieved by HMS *Glory,* after completing 64 days of operations during which 2,336 sorties were flown.

Soon after arriving on station, the engineers aboard the carrier undertook the experimental installation of two F.24 cameras in a modified drop

This side-on view of a Sea Fury shows the purposeful but clean lines of the type. (Fleet Air Arm Museum)

tank in an effort to restore some form of reconnaissance capability to the Sea Fury. The cameras were mounted at the front and rear of the tank, giving some panoramic facility to the setup. Although not adopted on a fleetwide basis, HMS *Glory* did use it throughout the carrier's tour.

Another innovation adopted by the Sea Fury squadron was the replacement of the rocket projectiles by 500-lb. bomb mounts. This requirement had arisen because the 60-lb. warhead had been found ineffective against some targets. Thus the Sea Fury became a dive bomber, and a

Overflying HMS Formidable, *this Sea Fury Mk.X was regarded as a lead in type by the Fleet Air Arm before the arrival of the more capable FB.11* (Fleet Air Arm Museum)

Seen from a head-on view, this shot of a T.Mk.20 shows the commonality of parts between both versions of the type. (Fleet Air Arm Museum)

very accurate one. These weapons had their fuses set at a 30-second delay, which allowed the pilot enough time to clear the drop zone. On 18 April, HMS *Glory* began its final patrol off the Korean coast before withdrawing in May.

To replace HMS *Glory*, the Royal Navy dispatched the fleet carrier

HMS *Ocean*, which was home to the First CAG. The units composing this air group were No. 802 Squadron, which was equipped with Sea Furies, and No. 805 Squadron, which flew the Firefly. It was during the period that HMS *Glory* was on station that the first enemy jet fighters began to make their presence felt. These were MiG-15s, which

were reported to have both Chinese and Russian pilots at various times, although all bore the insignia of the North Korean Air Force.

The first encounter between the jets and the piston-powered fighters of the Fleet Air Arm took place in the summer of 1952, when a flight of MiG-15s managed to slip through

This line-up of Sea Furies belong to No. 802 Squadron. The location is Hal Far in Malta. Within weeks the FB.11s would be aboard HMS Ocean on their way to Korea. (W A Harrison Collection)

This view of the port side of a Sea Fury parked on the grass at RNAS Lee on Solent shows the location of the pitot head on the wing (C P Russell Smith Collection)

the F-86 Sabre defensive line of the U.S. Air Force. A flight of Sea Furies from No. 802 Squadron were on patrol, when they were bounced by the jet fighters. The naval aircraft led by Lieutenant P. Carmicheal turned toward their attackers, all opening fire on the one aircraft that passed their gunsights. Hits were made on the Russian aircraft, which was seen to dive away with smoke pouring from it. Further entanglements saw Lieutenant Carmicheal placing a good burst on another Korean aircraft, which went down streaming smoke and flames before crashing. Other members of the flight had limited chances to take shots at the enemy aircraft. Even so, they eventually broke away, with two of their number lost and others damaged. The flight of Sea Furies did not get off lightly, however, as one burst of cannon fire struck the wing of one

Wearing the codes of HMS Theseus this FB.11 sports only underwing fuel tanks and rocket rails. (C P Russell Smith Collection)

This Sea Fury T.Mk.20 is unusually equipped with rocket rails, a feature rarely seen on this version. (W A Harrison Collection)

Originally the two-seat trainer had separate canopies, although this layout was changed when the rear one collapsed on the prototype. (C P Russell Smith Collection)

Sea Fury T.Mk.20 VX287 is parked alongside its single-seat counterpart. This version had only two cannons so the correct center of gravity could be maintained. (C P Russell Smith Collection)

This Sea Fury is parked up, awaiting disposal. Weathering has brought out the panel lines on the fuselage. (W A Harrison Collection)

aircraft, setting the wing alight. Skillful piloting and a severe side slip put out the fire and allowed the damaged Sea Fury to limp back to the carrier, where it made a safe landing. Further entanglements between the squadron and its jet-powered opposition took place later that week, although of the eight MiG-15s, only one was confirmed as damaged.

When HMS *Glory* resumed its duties on station off the Korean Coast, it was set to be the longest serving of all the fleet carriers assigned to the war. During this period, No. 810 Squadron and its extended complement of Sea Furies replaced those of the previous incumbent No. 804 Squadron. Meanwhile the other front line units operating the Hawker fighter were also to experience combat service during this period. Nos. 805 and 808 Squadrons did not fly from the carriers of the Royal Navy. Instead they were added to the strength of Australian carrier HMAS *Sydney* in consecutive order.

Regarding HMS *Glory*, while in theater, the carrier's air group flew nearly 30,000 sorties, during which a total of only 22 aircrew members were killed in action. This was a remarkably low figure, given the heavily defended targets they were sent to attack. Supplying the on-station fleet carrier was the role assigned to the maintenance carriers HMS *Unicorn* and *Warrior*.

While the front line Fleet Air Arm units were experiencing the rigors of Korea, at home in the United Kingdom the second line squadrons of the Royal Naval Reserve were reequipping with the new Hawker fighter bomber. This process began in 1951 and allowed the retirement of the original equipment flown by

these units, the Supermarine Seafire F.17. The first unit to receive the new type was No. 1832 Squadron in August 1951, while based at RAF Station Benson. Further deliveries saw Nos.1831, 1833, 1834, 1835, and 1836 Squadrons from the same organization reequip. These squadrons were based at St. Merryn, home of 1831 and 1833 Squadrons, and at Benson, where 1834, 1835 and 1836 Squadrons were based. Both stations had at least 27 Sea Furies allocated, although none were individually operated by the squadrons, all being pooled. Also sent to the reserve units was the greater majority of the Sea Fury T.20s, of which 60 were constructed by the manufacturer.

Deliveries to the Fleet Air Arm began in mid-1950, with one of the earliest being dispatched to the Naval Air Fighting Development Unit, which received VX283 for in-depth evaluation. The remaining trainers were spread out between Nos. 1831, 1832, 1833, 1834, 1835, and 1836 Squadrons RNVR. As they were not equipped with arrestor hooks, the T.20s were confined to shore-based training, although they did sport folding wings and a limited weapons capability.

Once operations in the Far East had concluded, the front line Sea Fury units began to relinquish their aircraft. The first to change its equipment was No. 803 Squadron, which began to equip with the Supermarine Attacker F.1 during November 1951. Further replacements saw No. 803 Squadron changing to the Attacker, after which it joined with No. 800 Squadron to become the air group aboard the revamped HMS *Eagle*. Thus passed the last, and possibly most capable, fighter bomber from the service of the Fleet Air Arm.

Bramcote was where most redundant Sea Furies were stored before either being scrapped or sold on by Hawker. This machine has its rudder and elevators held in place by external locks. (C P Russell Smith Collection)

Once on the inventory of 1834 Squadron RNVR VX637 is in store awaiting its fate. Although the wing fold jacks have safety locks fitted, it would appear that those for the flight controls are not. (C P Russell Smith Collection)

Parked in a hangar at Anthorn, these Sea Furies are sitting with their flaps fully down. Most are undergoing spares recovery. (C P Russell Smith Collection)

One of the aircraft put forward to replace the Sea Fury was the Westland Wyvern, which was optimized for fighter and torpedo delivery duties. This is the first version the TF.1. (Nick Challoner)

The service version of the Wyvern was the TF.4, which saw its own share of combat service over Suez. Unlike the earlier Sea Fury, this aircraft was powered by a Double Mamba turboprop. (C P Russell Smith Collection)

The last naval product produced by Hawker Aircraft as an independent company was the Sea Hawk jet fighter. (Big Bird Aviation Collection)

SEA FURY COLORS

A s the Hawker Sea Fury was conceived and ordered during the closing stages of World War II, it is no surprise to find that the first aircraft delivered for service with the Fleet Air Arm wore the standard upper surface finish of extra dark sea gray with sky under surfaces. This color scheme saw the Sea Fury F. Mk. X darkly colored down to the lower fuselage line. Codes were white while serial numbers and Royal Navy titles were painted black. Emergency, servicing, and technical instructions were also in black.

The entry into service of the more capable FB.11 saw the upper surface color shrinking upward to the upper fuselage line. Other markings remained the same color, although the roundels were changed from Type "B" to Type "C" and the fin flash finally disappeared from use across the aircraft of the Fleet Air Arm. Those aircraft assigned to operations in Korea had black and white striping applied to the wing lower surfaces and in sections on the upper and lower fuselage. Close observation of some of these Sea Furies would show that the lines were not as straight as portrayed by some sources.

In total contrast, the T.Mk. 20 trainers were delivered in a silver paint-

The Sea Furies diverted to the Royal Australian Navy were delivered in the same colors that were applied to the FAA machines. Their final color scheme, dark blue and sky, is shown here. (Nick Challoner)

ed lacquer finish overall, with many sporting trainer yellow identification bands. Serials and other identifying marks were as before, in black.

Overseas users such as Australia and Canada retained their Sea Furies in similar color schemes as applied to the machines of the Fleet Air Arm. Only the roundels changed, with those of Australia sporting a Kangaroo, while those of Canada wore the Maple Leaf. In Europe the Royal Netherlands Navy accepted its Sea Furies in similar finishes to those of the FAA. Later in their service, these aircraft and those of Australia wore a dark blue overall finish.

In the Middle East, the Furies delivered to the Egyptian Air Force were painted in overall silver lacquer, with green and white national markings. Identification and other markings were, as usual, black. Their close neighbors in Iraq accepted their airframes resplendent in a dark earth and stone finish with azure blue under surfaces. National

markings were carried in the usual places, with other markings in black. A similar color scheme was also applied to the Sea Furies sold to Pakistan.

Those aircraft sold to the Union of Burma were delivered wearing an overall silver scheme with national markings on the wing, fuselage, and fin. Those sold to Cuba were painted by Hawker with dark upper surfaces with lighter colored under surfaces. With the fall of the Batista regime, the markings originally applied were roughly overpainted with those of the FAR. In contrast, the German civilian target tugs were delivered in a bright red scheme that covered the whole airframe and identified them to enthusiastic gunners as target tugs.

Civilian machines, on the other hand, have flown in such a proliferation of schemes that to describe them would need a book in itself; therefore, let the photographs speak for themselves.

The Sea Fury T.Mk.20 was delivered in an overall silver finish and had trainer yellow bands applied to denote its status. The "GN" code pertains to RNAS Eglinton in Northern Ireland. (Nick Challoner)

The Iraqi single-seat Fury or ISS and its two-seat trainer equivalent were all painted in a color scheme designed for desert use. (Big Bird Aviation Collection)

The Sea Furies sold to the Royal Netherlands Navy ended their days in an overall dark blue finish, with white numbers and codes. (Big Bird Aviation Collection)

Flying past the camera, FB.11 VR930 reveals the full extent of its Korean striping. (Damien Burke)

Resplendent in Fleet Air Arm colors and Korean markings, preserved Sea Fury FB.11 VR930 begins its takeoff run. (Damien Burke)

Sea Furies purchased by Germany were reworked and operated by a civilian firm as target tugs, a role for which they were painted bright red overall. (Thomas Genth)

Sea Fury FB.11 VR930 is the example preserved in the Fleet Air Arm Museum at Yeovilton. It is fully restored in the markings applied to the type during the Korean War. (Damien Burke)

With the seat fully raised the pilot of this Sea Fury attempts to see his way forward, even so he will still have to weave the aircraft for a better view. (Nick Challenor)

With its flaps in the fully down position this RAN bedecked Sea Fury is caught just at the moment of touchdown. (Nick Challoner)

Dennis Sanders turned the pylons in Race No. 114, "Argonaut" in 1999. Sanders placed third in the Unlimited Silver, finishing at an average speed of 391.009 mph. (Nicholas A. Veronico)

Tom Dwelle taxies T.Mk.20S WE820, N85SF, "Critical Mass" out for the Unlimited Gold race in September 1996. Dwelle qualified at 397.735 mph. (Nicholas A. Veronico)

The Sanders family has been a racing dynasty since the family brought the Sea Fury T.Mk.20 VZ368, N20SF, "Dreadnought" to the Reno races in 1983. The R-4360 powered Sea Fury qualified at 446.392 mph and won the Unlimited Gold at 425.242 mph on its first outing with Neil Anderson at the controls. September 1994. Here, the Dreadnought crew prepares to launch the aircraft with Dennis Sanders at the controls for the 1994 Unlimited Gold Race. "Dreadnought" finished second at 416.632 mph. (Nicholas A. Veronico)

Bill Rheinschild's Race No. 74 "Bad Attitude" placed fifth in the Unlimited Silver race on September 19, 1999. (Nicholas A. Veronico)

Riff Raff, Race No. 99, flown by Robert "Hoot" Gibson qualified at 389.3960 mph in 1999. Gibson placed fourth in the Silver race that year averaging 390.624 mph. (Nicholas A. Veronico)

Howard Pardue's Fury FB.10, N666HP, Race No. 66, taxies past the Reno home pylon at the 1995 races. Pardue qualified at an average speed of 409.327 mph. He made it into the Unlimited Gold Race, but only completed six laps, at an average speed of 389.131 mph, before the race ended. (Nicholas A. Veronico)

In 1996, both Lloyd Hamilton and C.J. Stephens flew FB.Mk.11 WH857, N260X, Race Number 16, "Baby Gorilla." Hamilton qualified the Sea Fury at 374.056 mph, and flew it to a fifth place finish in the Unlimited Gold race at an average speed of 351.795 mph. Hamilton first brought the Sea Fury to the National Championship Air Races in 1972. (Nicholas A. Veronico)

This preserved Sea Fury wears the dark blue paint finish associated with the type's last years of service with the Royal Netherlands Navy. (W.A. Harrison Collection)

VZ345 was a Sea Fury T.Mk. 20 that was operated by A&AEE before being damaged in an accident. (Big Bird Aviation Collection)

A pure diorama photograph, as Sea Fury D-CATA is refueled after its flight. (Thomas Genth)

IN STRA**6**GE SEAS

In light of its reasonable overseas sales record, Hawker Aircraft must have done something right during its intensive sales drive. The first overseas customer was to be the Royal Netherlands Navy, which placed an order on 21 October 1946 under contract N/SF/2001 for 10 Sea Fury F.50 fighters, which were basically equivalent to the Fleet Air Arm's F Mk. X. These were given the serial numbers 10-1 to 10-10 for service aboard the Royal Navy light carrier HMS *Nairana*. The operating unit was No. 860 Squadron, which had originally been a Fleet Air Arm unit number, although the numberplate was transferred to the Netherlands Navy after 1945. No. 860 Squadron carried out its unit work up at RNAS St. Merryn before flying out to the carrier. Not long after this event, HMS *Nairina* was transferred to the Netherlands Navy as the HrMs *Karel Doorman*. Although a separate entity, the ships of the Netherlands Navy frequently operated alongside their Royal Navy counterparts. Thus it was not unusual to see Dutch Sea Furies operating from Fleet Air Arm land bases and carriers. During 1947, the Sea Furies of No. 860 Squadron operated from the HrMs *Karel Doorman* in support of ground forces attacking insurgent guerrillas in the Dutch East Indies. The fleet carrier was returned to the Royal Navy in 1948 for return to its original civilian role. The Sea Fury F.50s remained in front line service with No. 860 Squadron until 18 March 1950.

This situation only lasted until 15 July 1950, when the unit was reformed by the simple expedient of redesignating the *Gevechtsvliegopleiding* or the Fighter Pilots Combat School. Based at Valkenburg, this unit was equipped with the Hawker Sea Fury FB.50, which was equal to the Sea Fury FB.11 of the Fleet Air Arm. The contract for this particular batch of airframes, which totaled 12, had been placed on 12 January 1950 as N/SF/3001. The carrier destined to be the seagoing base for the squadron was the HrMs *Karel Doorman*, second carrier with this name, which had been purchased from the Royal Navy, where it had been HMS *Venerable*, on 1 April 1948. A further batch of Sea Fury FB.50s was constructed by Fokker in Holland, which brought the total up to 48 airframes. No. 860 Squadron continued to fly the Sea Fury FB.50 until disbanding on 15 June 1956, after which its aircraft were transferred to No. 3 Squadron of the Netherlands Navy. The replacement for the Sea Fury was another Hawker product, the jet-powered Sea Hawk.

Another wartime ally, the Royal Canadian Navy, which had become a separate service from the RCAF in 1945, also purchased the Sea Fury. These were delivered between 1948 and 1951 and totaled 35 overall. No individual contract for these aircraft was issued, as they were diverted from Royal Navy contracts. The operational units slated to fly the new RCN fighter were No. 883 Squadron allocated to the Eighteenth CAG and No. 803 Squadron of the Nineteenth CAG. The first air-

Flying low over the sea, this Sea Fury of the Royal Netherlands Navy heads toward the carrier Karel Doorman. The first airframes supplied to Holland were ex-FAA, thus few changes were made to the original equipment. (Fleet Air Arm Museum)

Seen on approach to Luqa, Malta, this RNN FB.11 has its flaps in the fully down position as it begins its landing approach. (C P Russell Smith Collection)

frame was accepted on 23 June 1948 at the Royal Canadian Air Force base at Rockliffe.

The Royal Canadian Navy had gained its first aircraft carrier, HMS *Warrior*, in January 1946. Originally its air group had been equipped with Supermarine Seafires and Fairey Fireflies before reequipping. When the Sea Furies arrived, so did a replacement aircraft carrier, this being the Majestic class vessel HMCS *Magnificent*, more commonly known as the *Maggie*. The new fight-er's primary role was to provide fleet air defense and air cover for the antisubmarine Fairey Fireflies. As delivered, the Sea Furies of the RCN were able to tote the same weaponry as their Fleet Air Arm equivalents. Thus each carried four cannons plus mounts for external fuel tanks, rocket projectiles, 500-lb. bombs, and 1,000-lb. bombs.

Before assuming an active service role with the RCN, the carrier HMCS *Magnificent* had spent a period working up to full operational strength at Eglinton, Northern Ireland, before proceeding across the Atlantic with the aircraft of the Nineteenth CAG aboard. Once in Canadian territorial waters the aircraft of the Nineteenth CAG remained aboard the carrier, while the aircraft assigned to the Eighteenth CAG were transferred to the RCAF Joint Air School at Rivers, Manitoba, for further specialized training after departing from the carrier.

In September 1948 the Cabinet Defense Committee decided to transfer the base at Manitoba to the RCN, which subsequently renamed it Shearwater. During the same month the aircraft of the Nineteenth CAG came ashore from HMCS *Magnificent* while the Sea Furies of Eighteenth CAG completed their training. A further period of training then followed for the Eighteenth CAG. This took place at the U.S. Naval base at Quonset Point, where it was to undergo conversion to U.S. Navy deck landing practices, a decision that was to affect both the RN and the RCN. Much of this centered upon approach procedures as practiced by both navies, which required a uniform approach height during the landing circuit before descending at a steady rate from 400 feet. In contrast, the U.S. Navy flew a gently descending turn before being signaled by the deck landing officer to cut engines just prior to touchdown. Converting to this new method caused problems, as pilots had a tendency to land on the main undercarriages instead of a more tail-down angle. As the main gear designed for British carrier aircraft was stressed for a more tail-down landing, this new method began to cause airframe overstress and damage to the mountings. Another problem encountered was the bounceback as the undercar-

In common with its FAA counterparts, the RNN used locks to stop the folded wings from spreading accidentally. The landing light on the folded portion of the wing is prominent. (C P Russell Smith Collection)

riage reacted to the compression, frequently resulting in the aircraft clearing the arrestor wires completely.

In a change to the original ship's complement, the operating unit aboard the HMCS *Magnificent* was changed to the Eighteenth CAG, while the Nineteenth CAG remained ashore for training duties. This cruise was not without incident, as a Sea Fury ended up crashing into the sea after engine failure, although the pilot was rescued. This loss notwithstanding, the Eighteenth CAG continued its exercise flying, the primary point of which was to intercept a target ship, HMS *Jamaica*, which was sailing from the Canal Zone to Jamaica. Patrolling Sea Furies found the ship some 210 miles from the carrier. They returned to the *Maggie,* refueled, and returned over a distance of 162 miles to carry out a simulated strike before returning to their floating airfield.

In December 1949, the Royal Cana-

This FB.11 of the Netherlands Navy, which sports an unusual tail hook lock, is parked for an overnight stop (W A Harrison Collection)

dian Navy decided to rewrite the record books, using a pair of Sea Furies from No. 883 Squadron. Their mission was to fly from Toronto, Ontario, to Halifax, Nova Scotia, in the shortest possible time. Departure was from Malton Airport to RCNAS Dartmouth, the ensuing distance of 825 air miles being covered in one hour and 54 minutes, at an average ground speed of 435.35 mph.

As politicians are wont to do, the Canadian government decided to reorganize the aircraft and personnel of the RCN. The end result came to fruition in January 1951, with the Eighteenth CAG having Nos. 826 and 883 Squadrons assigned, while the Nineteenth CAG was renamed as a Support Air Group with Nos. 803 and 825 Squadrons making up its strength. As its name implies, the

Wearing the earlier dark sea gray and sky blue finish, this RNN Sea Fury is awaiting delivery from the Hawker airfield at Langley. (C P Russell Smith Collection)

Sea Fury 10-4 wears Kon Marine titles under the tailplane. The reflection of the light highlights the cannon breech blisters. (W A Harrison Collection)

SAG was to be land-based; thus its base became RCNAS Shearwater on a permanent basis. The aircraft of the Eighteenth CAG were to help christen the newly opened Chezzetcook Firing and Bombing Range before departing to Quonset Point for some presailing training. Once this was complete, the air component flew out to join HMCS *Magnificent*, which was sailing near Bermuda. Unfortunately, during this seagoing period, the group lost two Sea Furies and one pilot in accidents.

In May 1951 the squadrons of the RCN were renumbered to tie in with the Commonwealth numbering series. Thus the last wartime links with the FAA was to disappear. Nos. 803 and 825 were to become Nos. 870 and 880 Squadrons respectively and were the air component of the Thirty-first SAG. The renumbered Eighteenth CAG became the Thirtieth CAG, whose units were Nos. 871 and 881 Squadrons, instead of 883 and 826 Squadrons respectively. As the Thirtieth CAG needed to undergo night landing training prior to sailing aboard the *Maggie*, the Thirty-first SAG was to supply the air defense requirement until the squadrons were ready.

With the Thirtieth CAG aboard HMCS *Magnificent*, it took part in numerous night antisubmarine and CAP patrols, all of which were phases of Exercise Castinets. During these maneuvers, undertaken in European waters during June 1951, it achieved the highest flying hours

The Netherlands Navy always maintained its aircraft in excellent condition. Even the inside of the main gear doors are clean enough to see their method of construction. (W A Harrison Collection)

The Royal Canadian Navy also operated the Sea Fury. This example is preparing to depart on a test flight. (C P Russell Smith Collection)

of any Air Group. By July the carrier was in the Mediterranean, where it encountered some unseasonal weather. At least four Sea Furies were forced to divert to Aroxas Air Base, Greece, when the over-the-deck wind speed was to drop so low as to make landing hazardous. A few days later, the Sea Furies moved to Ellinikon, near Athens, from where they were to try again. Of the four approaches, two were successful while the third was to suffer a hydraulic failure. As there was no pressing case to land aboard the carrier, the damaged aircraft and the fourth Sea Fury returned to Ellinikon, where a blowdown of the requisite systems was carried out. HMCS *Magnificent* dispatched a repair crew aboard a Grumman Avenger, with instructions that all three aircraft were to meet up with the carrier group at Hal Far, Malta, on 27 July.

A move to the Atlantic to take part in Operation Main Brace took place in September 1952, and was scheduled to last 13 days. Aircraft from

the *Maggie* acted in concert with those from the Royal Navy Fleet Carrier HMS *Theseus* in daylight CAP and night antisubmarine

This Sea Fury FB.11, also operated by the RCN, is fitted with 45-gallon external fuel tanks. (C P Russell Smith Collection)

Diverted from an FAA contract, this Sea Fury FB.11 entered service with the RCN. Very few changes were made to these diverted aircraft, mainly concentrated on communications equipment. (W A Harrison Collection)

CAG were among the aircraft that took part in the flypast. While the Thirtieth CAG was taking part in the flypast, its opposite number, the Thirty-first SAG was vacating the air base at Shearwater, which was closing temporarily for major reconstruction. Its new home was to be RCAF Scoudouc in New Brunswick. However, this respite was shortlived as Scoudouc was scheduled to close, and a further move was undertaken to the RCAF Station at Summerside, Prince Edward Island.

patrols, before acting as top cover for exercise landings in northern Denmark. In the months that followed, the unit designations of the RCN squadrons were to change to mimic those of the U.S. Navy, thus No. 880 Squadron became VS 880.

In February 1953 the aircraft of the Thirtieth CAG were to be found operating from Rivers, Manitoba, taking part in a close air support operation entitled Exercise Assiniboine, after which the squadrons took part in a flag-waving exercise. By June, the Thirtieth CAG was embarked on HMCS *Magnificent* in transit for Spithead, for the Coronation Review Flypast. On 15 June eight Sea Furies from the Thirtieth

During the period that encompasses the war in Korea, the Sea Fury pilots were anxious to take part in the hostilities. The Canadian government stated that the carrier was not available for such duties, as its role was that of antisubmarine patrol, not attack. The fighters, however, were not covered by the same dictate. In any event, the Canadian carrier force was not dispatched to Korea. The alternative offered was Exercise Mariner,

This RCN FB.11 has a whip aerial fitted to the tip of the fin. (C P Russell Smith Collection)

VX690 is shown carrying both 60-gallon fuel tanks and rocket launch rails. This aircraft had been diverted from an FAA order to the RCN. (C P Russell Smith Collection)

The Canadian machines were in different states of modification; as VX686 has its whip aerial located behind the cockpit, rather than on the fin. (W A Harrison Collection)

Complete with late modification aerials and 45-gallon tanks, TG129 was part of No. 870 Squadron RCN. (W A Harrison Collection)

which involved 300 vessels and over 1,000 aircraft. As this was a NATO exercise, the two opposing forces were designated as blue and orange respectively. The Canadian carrier group was allocated to the blue force, regarded by many taking part as the good guys. The Sea Fury squadron VF 871 carried out the duties of antisubmarine patrol and defense against long-range aerial intruders.

Further operations and exercises were to occupy the aircraft and crew

of HMCS *Magnificent* until mid-1956. At that time, the Hawker Sea Furies were placed in storage, as they were being replaced by the RCN's first jets, the McDonnell F2H-3 Banshee. The last official flight of a Hawker Sea Fury in front line Royal Canadian Navy colors took place in early 1957, when aircraft WG565 was delivered to Reserve Air Squadron VG 924 based as Calgary, Alberta.

At the other end of the globe, further Hawker Sea Furies were diverted from Fleet Air Arm contracts to sat-

isfy the needs of the Royal Australian Navy. The first aircraft delivered, VW562, arrived in 1950 and was to be followed by 32 more. Operated by Nos. 805 and 808 Squadrons RAN, the Sea Furies were deployed aboard the RAN carrier *Sydney* and HMS *Vengeance* during the fighting in Korea. No. 805 Squadron had reformed at Eglinton in Northern Ireland upon receipt of 13 Sea Fury FB.11s. In February 1949, the ship and No. 805 Squadron departed the Atlantic for Australian waters. After service in Korea, the unit was deployed as a guard squadron to protect the Monte Bello Atomic Test Area. On 26 March 1958 the squadron arrived at the RAN station Nowra for disbandment. Its sister unit, No. 808 Squadron, formed with 13 Sea Fury FB.11s on 25 April 1950. In a similar manner to the earlier squadron, No. 808 Squadron flew from its formation base, in this case St. Merryn, to join the carrier HMAS *Sydney*, where it became part of the Twenty-first CAG. Service in Korean waters included a spell aboard the *Vengeance* as part of the Twenty-first CAG. Disbandment took place at RAN Nowra on 5 October 1954. The other front line unit to use the Sea Fury was No. 850 Squadron while in second line usage No. 724 Squadron was the training support unit. No. 850 Squadron received 12 Sea Fury FB.11s in January 1953 for service in the Korean theater of operations. The unit was shortlived, however, as it disbanded in August 1954. In 1958 the Sea Fury was replaced by the D H Sea Venom, although No. 724 Squadron flew a few examples until late 1962.

Other countries were to also operate the Sea Fury. Some were new build while others were refurbished ex-FAA machines. The furthest east of

Another Commonwealth country that flew the Sea Fury FB.11 was Australia, whose WZ643 is shown here. This was a standard airframe diverted from an FAA contract. (C P Russell Smith Collection)

After front line service, the Sea Furies of the RAN were used for second line duties. They also underwent some modification to the radio equipment, as the whip aerial on the fin shows. (C P Russell Smith Collection)

these nations was Burma, whose government was to order 18 aircraft. These were drawn from stocks that had been purchased by Hawker from the MoS, which had acted as the disposal agent for the ex-Royal Navy machines. Contract HAL/57/B./030 was issued to cover the refurbishment of these machines, all of which were of the FB.11 variety, although two were modified with target tow hooks, but without the winch. In this form they were variously designated the FB.11(TT) or TT.11. Serials for these aircraft were in the UB454 to UB471 range, and they were delivered throughout 1958. The single-seaters were followed by a batch of three T.20 trainers that were delivered during the same period. These

VW623 was an FB.11 that was preserved by the RAN at Nowra AB. As it was used for second line work after retirement from carrier duty, its arrestor hook has been removed. (C P Russell Smith Collection)

Sea Furies were serialed UB451 to UB453. Very little is known of their service use, although they are reported to have stayed in front line service until 1968, when they were replaced by the Lockheed T-33.

In the Middle East two countries were to operate the Hawker Sea Fury in quantity at various times. The first of these was Egypt, which

received its first single example during April/May 1948. This had been the prototype F2/43 Fury, which had been refurbished and had its original early engine replaced by an uprated Centaurus XVIII powerplant. The Fury was then repainted in civilian color and given the registration G-AKRY for ferrying purposes. Hawker Aircraft displayed the Fury to EAF leaders, who were

UB451 was an ex-FAA machine that was sold to the Union of Burma Air Force. As such they were basically unchanged from the original. (W A Harrison Collection)

enthusiastic about the aircraft and placed an order. This was suspended, due to the conflict between the Arab nations and the newly formed state of Israel. The British embargo only covered firms in the United Kingdom, which did not stop other countries supplying arms. Thus it was Iraq that supplied a pair of its Fury complement to bolster the Egyptian forces. At least one was destroyed during combat with the Israeli Air Force, and a similar fate is

thought to have befallen the other two. Once hostilities had been concluded, the Egyptian government placed an order for 12 Sea Fury FB.11s under contract 17/49/USS. They were delivered during 1950–1951. At least one was to be destroyed on the ground during the initial strikes that marked the opening of Operation Musketeer, the purpose of which was to recapture the Suez Canal during November/December 1956.

The other user of the Hawker fighter in the Middle East was Iraq, which placed its order for the type on 4 December 1946. This contract initially called for 30 single-seat fighters, designated by Hawker as ISS or Iraqi single-seaters, and four trainers, designated IDT or Iraqi dual-trainers, although this was later reduced to two. A further order was placed on 21 July 1951 for 15 new build ISS fighters. Ten refurbished ex-FAA Sea Fury FB.11s and three T.20s, ordered on 7 March 1953, were diverted from a Fleet Air Arm contract. Deliveries were undertaken during 1952 and 1953.

The delivery flights were undertaken on behalf of Hawker Aircraft by Airwork Ltd. Departure was from the company airfield at Langley and was routed via Blackbushe, Nice, Malta, Mersa Metruh, Nicosia, and on to a landing in Baghdad. As soon as each aircraft touched down, the waiting ground crew helped the pilot out of the cockpit, after which all the engine cowlings were opened to assist the cooling down of the powerplant. While in service, the Baghdad Furies were reportedly used in action against the Kurds in Northern Iraq. They were withdrawn from service starting in 1960 and placed in storage, from which a large cache was sold to an American consortium in the early 1970s.

Morocco acquired the Hawker Sea Fury on 4 February 1960 when a pair of Furies were presented as a gift by Iraq to the emergent Aviation Royale Cherifienne, which later evolved into the Royal Moroccan Air Force. Two more were delivered from the same source in late 1961. The four Furies saw little operational use, and eventually ended up in storage at Rabat. From there, they were sold to an American dealer.

WZ649 has its aerials under the center fuselage, installed there by the RAN. (C P Russell Smith Collection)

One of the largest export customers to purchase the Sea Fury was Pakistan. Formed on the country's independence in 1947, the new Pakistan Air Force had based much of its operational and service doctrine upon that of the Royal Air Force. Initially three of its fighter squadrons were equipped with another Hawker product, the Tempest.

To replace these elderly fighter bombers, the PAF ordered a total of 93 Furies. The first of these was the F2/43 Fury prototype, NX802, which was bought in March 1949 after refurbishment by Hawker. This single airframe was followed by 50 Furies, designated the F.60, which were ordered in 1950. A order for a further 24 was received in 1951 with another 13 being procured during 1951–1952. A further five single-seaters were converted from ex-FAA Sea Fury FB.11s, and arrived in Pak-

Complete with rudder clamp, this ISS Fury sits at Blackbushe, prior to undertaking its delivery flight. (C P Russell Smith Collection)

istan in 1953–1954. The conversion aspect was covered by the purchase of five trainers, designated the T.61, one of which was diverted from the Iraqi contract while the others were new built.

In service, the Furies equipped Nos. 5 and 9 Squadrons PAF in 1950 with No. 14 Squadron following suit during the following year. To support the Fury, which was the primary weapon in the PAF, No. 2 Fighter

This silver-finished FB.11 was one of a quantity Hawker sold to Burma after purchasing them from the MoS. (W A Harrison Collection)

Seen awaiting delivery from Blackbushe is this Fury destined for the Iraqi Air Force. It would appear that it was once an ex-Naval example as there is a fairing for an arrestor hook to the rear of the tail wheel. (C P Russell Smith Collection)

Conversion School at Maripur also received some Fury F.60s for training purposes. The Fury remained in front line service until 1955, when the piston fighters were replaced in the inventories of Nos. 5 and 14 Squadrons by the North American F-86 Sabre. The remaining operational unit, No. 9 Squadron, held onto its Furies until 1960, as they were ideally suited for the assigned role, that of policing the northwest frontier. The conversion unit also relinquished its aircraft in 1955, these being replaced by Lockheed T-33 trainers delivered under MAP auspices. As for No. 9 Squadron, it received another Lockheed product, the F-104 Starfighter. The final handful of Furies to be withdrawn were finally grounded in 1963 after duties as target towers.

With its pilot aboard, an Iraqi ISS Fury prepares to depart from Nicosia Cyprus for its final destination, Baghdad. (W A Harrison Collection)

In the Americas, apart from Canada, only Cuba was to be a customer for the Hawker Sea Furies. This order was fulfilled by Hawker using refurbished ex-FAA Sea Fury FB.11s and T.20s. Totals of these were respectively 15 and two, ordered in 1957 with deliveries occurring during 1958. Intended for the Cuban Air Force, these aircraft were crated and delivered by sea. As the country of Cuba and the Batista government were beset by internal strife, exceptional precautions were taken to protect the newly arrived Furies. As they were unloaded at Havana, the workers were closely observed, even though they had been thoroughly searched before starting work. Although a handful of aircraft had been erected, they were not able

541 is one of two Sea Furies preserved in Cuba. This example has inert rockets under the wings. (Fleet Air Arm Museum)

L982 is a Fury destined for service with the Pakistani Air Force. In this view the pilot's access stirrup is extended and the aircraft sports underwing fuel tanks needed for its delivery flight. (C P Russell Smith Collection)

Possibly the strangest looking version of the Sea Fury was the Iraqi Air Force two seat trainer that originally featured this double canopy ensemble. Problems with cavitation in the rear cockpit eventually led to the adoption of the assembly seen on the T.Mk.20 for the Fleet Air Arm. (Hawker Aircraft)

Complete with underwing fuel tanks, this Fury (L951) is awaiting delivery to the Pakistani Air Force. (C P Russell Smith Collection)

to support the Batista government forces due to a lack of armament. On 1 January 1959, the forces of Fidel Castro overthrew the Batista regime and assumed control of Cuba and its aircraft.

The change of government meant the suspension of an order that encompassed a further 10 Sea Furies, a large quantity of bombs, rocket projectiles, and cannon shells. These items were never delivered.

Another consequence of the overthrow was the purging of the air force, which finally left 43 pilots available to fly the country's aircraft. Further negotiations were undertaken by Castro's representatives with Hawker to finalize the equipping of the Sea Furies with cannon and to provide the required ammunition. Eventually a force of some 12 aircraft were declared operational in November 1959. However, this state of affairs did not last long, as their batteries were stolen during an internal power struggle within the Cuban air force. In an effort to bring

The Royal Australian Navy was also a Sea Fury operator as the RAN titling on the rear fuselage indicates. In this view all the access footsteps are open to the cockpit. (C P Russell Smith Collection)

From any angle the Hawker Sea Fury is a mighty beast as this view of an Australian marked version shows. (Nick Challenor)

the Sea Furies up to a serviceable state, Hawker dispatched a team of engineers to repair the aircraft under a contract originally set at six months in length. Further trouble was to beset the Fuerza Aerea Revolucionaria when yet another purge of aircrew was carried out. This left the FAR with a total of six pilots, who were supplemented by others from Chile. During these events in June 1960, only the Hawker team was available to maintain the aircraft. With good spares support from Langley, they were able to keep all 12 flyable.

On 15 April 1961 a force of B-26B Invaders painted in FAC markings and crewed by Cuban exiles attacked the base at La Libertad, where one Sea Fury was destroyed on the ground. A further aircraft was

Seen from underneath, the shape of the Sea Fury's wings is fully revealed. Close observation will show the layout of the undersurface panels. (Nick Challenor)

Parked on the flight line are this gaggle of Sea Furies of the Royal Canadian Navy awaiting delivery to the carrier HMCS Magnificent. (C P Russell Smith Collection)

Caught during a transit stop is this Iraqi Fury destined to land at Baghdad a few hours later. Access to all Furies was via the steps on the left hand side. (C P Russell Smith Collection)

destroyed later in the day. Once the attacks had ceased, only four Sea Furies remained flyable, although this total eventually reduced to three being based at San Antonio AB. However this resource was not wasted, as the aircraft started operations against the invading forces, mainly strafing the troops on the beach. Following on from these early missions, Sea Fury FAR 541 attacked the supply ship Houston with rocket projectiles, sinking it. During these exchanges, one of the surviving Sea Furies, FAR 542, was shot down.

With the cessation of hostilities, the two surviving Sea Furies flew intermittently before being finally replaced in June 1961 by a large force of MiG-15s. Both survivors reside in Cuban museums.

The Bay of Pigs fiasco was to be the final battle for the Sea Fury throughout the world.

At the end of its landing run this Sea Fury, complete with passenger in the rear seat, rolls out with its flaps fully deployed. The rear seat is an extra addition fitted during its warbird days. (Nick Challenor)

WARBIRD**TECH**
SERIES

PRIVATE SEA FURIES

RACERS AND TARGET CHASERS

The first organization to entertain the Sea Fury, outside of Hawker Aircraft, which purchased many for export, was a German organization: the Deutsche Luftfahrt Beratungsdienst. The order for these ex-FAA aircraft was placed in 1958 with deliveries occurring between 1958 and 1960. Prior to entering service in Germany, one of the 10 T.Mk. 20s was used to trial the target winch installation. This was an air-driven system with the generator placed on the starboard side of the aircraft. The cable guides fed out under the fuselage and incorporated a cable cutter, lest there be a cable snarl, although tailplane protection wires were installed to reduce the possibility of entanglement. The remainder of the fleet had the Swiss-made equipment installed upon arrival in Germany. Once the initial contract had been fulfilled, another order directed to the MoS was placed for Hawker to deliver a further six airframes. All were refurbished ex-Fleet Air Arm machines.

After delivery, the red-painted target tugs were based at Lubeck, Cologne, or Bonn and were contracted to the Luftwaffe to provide towed targets for both naval and artillery gunners. They were later joined by an ex-Royal Netherlands Navy single-seater FB.11 for similar duties. While in service, five were lost in crashes before retirement in 1970, some possibly due to carbon monoxide poisoning. The surviving two-seaters were sold off to new owners while the single-seater is on display in the Luftwaffenmuseum at Uetersen.

Their replacements were a fleet of brand new North American OV-10 Broncos, which were operated by the Luftwaffe, although these too are now retired. The registrations of the DLB fleet were D-CABY, D-CACA, D-CACE, D-CACI, D-CACO, D-CACU, D-CIBO, D-CAMI, D-CATA, D-COTE, D-CCCO, D-CEBO, D-CABU, D-CADA, and D-CAFO, with the FB.11 being registered D-CACY.

The T.Mk. 20s were sold on to new owners. Three returned to the UK to resume military marks. Two of these are under the care of the RNHF, while the other, VZ345, resumed a flying career with the A&AEE at Boscombe Down. Unfortunately, it was badly damaged in a landing accident at Boscombe Down on 17

A German company, Deutsche Luftfahrt Beratungsdienst, purchased a quantity of Sea Fury T.Mk.20s for the purpose of target towing. This is D-CABY seen without its winch assembly. (W A Harrison Collection)

D-COTE, in common with the other German T.Mk.20s, was equipped with 45-gallon underwing fuel tanks. (W A Harrison Collection)

April 1985. The cause was later attributed to excess braking on landing, which caused the aircraft not only to stand on its nose, but to flip over on its back. Although the damage was repairable, it was decided to use the aircraft for spares in the repair of FB.11 VR930 at the British Aerospace factory in Brough, Humberside, as funding was not available for rebuilding. Four others were purchased by a British buyer and were based at Blackbushe before being sold to various buyers in the United States. Two others also reached the United States via another buyer, this time in Belgium, although they were in a very derelict condition. Direct sales would account for the remainder of the fleet.

The United States has the biggest collection of ex-service Sea Furies and Furies in the world. The sources for these are numerous, although the UK and Iraq, ironically, have been the biggest providers. The former has provided 12 examples, both fighters and trainers, while the latter was responsible for at least 20 airframes, although only one is a two-seater. At least three others are extant in the UK, coming from Australia, Canada, and Morocco. The airframe from Morocco has been very elusive to locate.

And the reason for this great number? The great sport of pylon air racing, which is exemplified by the

DLB procured one single FB.11 for target towing. D-CACY was the example, and like the others, was equipped with 45-gallon fuel tanks. (W A Harrison Collection)

D-CAMI was also delivered to DLB for target towing. The guides for the target cable are seen under the fuselage. (W A Harrison Collection)

Reno Races. Whatever they look like on the outside, these airframes are far from stock under the skin. To some degree or other they have all been tweaked to improve performance. Some changes are purely structural, whilst others are extremely radical and aerodynamic in nature. Others are, of course, for maintenance reasons. Pratt & Whitney R-3350 engines are replacing the Bristol Centaurus engine, as spares are becoming increasingly hard to obtain for the British engine, and large quantities of the American powerplant are more readily available. With the change of powerplant, the original five-blade Rotol propeller assembly is replaced by an American-built Hamilton Standard unit.

One of the machines that exemplifies the American approach is NX85SF, which has undergone a massive rebuild. Changes include a completely new tailplane shortened by two feet, and both fin and rudder squared off in appearance. Great alterations were also made to the fuselage, where the cockpit has been reduced to the smallest possible size and a fairing has been introduced that runs from the pilot's headrest to the base of the fin. The pilot's cockpit is actually located in the rear position, as this is an ex-T.Mk. 20 two-seat trainer, which had been operated by the Fleet Air Arm and later DLB in Germany. Covering the original front cockpit is aluminum plating, which is faired into the engine cowling. The engine itself is now a Wright R-3350 Double Cyclone, tweaked up to 4,000 horsepower. This particular engine once graced the wing of a Douglas B-26

At least one Fury flies in the UK, representing the Iraqi ISS version. (Nick Challoner)

WH588 is a privately owned Sea Fury that represents the RAN. Only the modern avionics aerial under the fuselage betrays the time period. (Nick Challoner)

Invader, although it now drives a four-bladed Aero Products propeller.

Although not strikingly obvious, the wings have also undergone drastic changes. The span has dropped by more than six feet to exactly 32 feet. Under the skin, the former gun bays now house coolant radiators for the powerplant. All these changes have not increased the level speed greatly, as the aircraft managed a shade under 430 mph in the Reno 2000 qualifiers; the extra performance is appreciated in the pylon turns.

Other countries also have a few flying examples. Australia has one based in Perth, and an ex-Iraqi ISS graces the skies of airshows such as Wanaka, New Zealand. Both are close to original build standard, without armament. Besides the numerous flying examples, airframes are in various museums around the world. Some are more accessible than others. For the historian and enthusiast, one of the easiest to get close too is the Sea Fury FB.11 in the Fleet Air Arm Museum at Yeovilton, Somerset, UK.

Thus after an illustrious service career, the surviving Sea Furies bring pleasure to many people within the aviation sphere.

When the Sea Fury was towed out of the hangar, a towing bridle was attached to the center launch point, and a steering arm was fitted to the tail wheel. (Thomas Genth)

These German T.Mk.20 target tugs are lined up to be prepared for flight. Close observation of the second aircraft shows the air-driven winch under the canopy. (Thomas Genth)

VH-BOU is a Sea Fury that is maintained in flying condition in Australia. It sports 45-gallon underwing tanks, but lacks an arrestor hook. (W A Harrison Collection)

To jack up the Sea Fury, the external fuel tanks needed to be removed, as shown on this DLB Sea Fury. (Thomas Genth)

This over-the-top shot of a DLB Sea Fury shows much of the upper wing access panel detail, as well as the winch. Even though these aircraft were unarmed, the original breech access panel was retained after conversion. (Thomas Genth)

The wing fold mechanism of the Sea Fury was put to good use by DLB, as it allowed the company to store more aircraft under cover. (Thomas Genth)

This slightly off-center head-on shot clearly shows the location of the target winch cable guide. (Thomas Genth)

All Sea Furies with their wings folded seemed to have their ailerons relax in a similar manner. This was not unusual, as the control of these surfaces was via the tab and not by direct connection. (Thomas Genth)

Slung from a mobile crane, this Centaurus engine has just been removed from the Sea Fury in the background and will be placed in the cradle just behind it (Thomas Genth)

Five aircraft of the DLB fleet are lined up here awaiting their next sortie. All are equipped with 45-gallon fuel tanks and target winches. (Thomas Genth)

When the number of aircraft requiring hangar space was low, they were put away with their wings spread. Note the drip tray under the fuselage to catch wayward fluid leaks. (Thomas Genth)

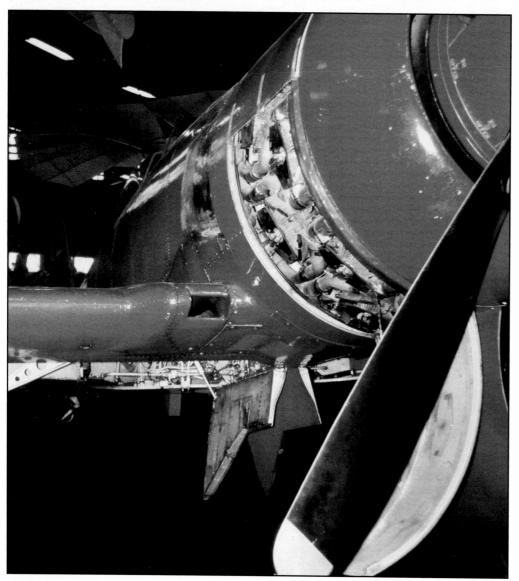

When the engine cowlings for the Centaurus were opened, they were held in place by integral stays to allow for safe access. (Thomas Genth)

Although the deflector plate helped direct the exhaust clear of the airframe, inevitably some swept back over the fuselage, as the state of the burnt paint shows. (Thomas Genth)

With cowlings, spinner, and propeller assembly removed, this Centaurus undergoes repair on the flightline. (Thomas Genth)

The crane is supporting the propeller assembly and engine front plate prior to it being installed on the waiting aircraft. (Thomas Genth)

One last check before the winch dolly is moved to the Sea Fury. Careful maneuvering will be needed to guide the assembly onto the splined drive without damaging it. (Thomas Genth)

Seen from behind is T Mk.20 D-CABY awaiting its pilot. Of note is the power supply lead plugged in under the fuselage. It should be noted that the Sea Furies were normally crewed by just a pilot, the second seat remaining empty. (C P Russell Smith Collection)

Doing what it does best, a German Sea Fury with a target under tow. (Thomas Genth)

A DLB Sea Fury in immaculate condition taxies out for a target towing sortie. When they finally retired, these excellent aircraft were replaced by the North American OV-10 Bronco, operated by the Luftwaffe. (Thomas Genth)

This shot from behind illustrates the target towing winch and the protective wires that guard the tailplane. (Thomas Genth)

Complete with fixed tail wheel is this ex-military Sea Fury T.20 whose distinctive canopy arrangement is shown here. (C P Russell Smith Collection)

Surrounded by more modern hardware is Sea Fury N232 which is preserved in America. This angle reveals the humped look of the fighters fuselage whose apex is at the cockpit. (C P Russell Smith Collection)

N878M had once been a frontline fighter before the American air racing specialist got their hands on it. Changes to the airframe includes a canopy of a reduced size and squared off wingtips that indicate a reduced wing span. (C P Russell Smith Collection)

N195F is a Hawker Sea Fury immaculately finished in the markings of the Royal Canadian Navy. As the aircraft operates from shore bases only, the arrestor hook has been removed. (C P Russell Smith Collection)

Cotton mouth *features modified canopies to improve its aerodynamic behavior, a feature not required during its aircrew training days.* (C P Russell Smith Collection)

Hitched to a towing vehicle is this Sea Fury which wears the markings of the Royal Australian Navy. N588 features a truncated arrestor hook assembly. (C P Russell Smith Collection)

Pardue's Number 66 Sea Fury is a consistent competitor. In 1996, Pardue qualified at 406.794 mph, a little less than 3 mph slower than the previous year. In 1996, Pardue flew No. 66 to a second place finish in the Unlimited Silver race at an average speed of 374.778 mph. (Nicholas A. Veronico)

Resplendent in a startling black and yellow trim is this Sea Fury pictured at Miami in 1973. (C P Russell Smith Collection)

G-FURY is a retired FAA Sea Fury which was a display favorite in the UK when this portrait was taken in 1980. (C P Russell Smith Collection)

GLOSSARY

AAA	Anti Aircraft Artillery		PAF	Pakistan Air Force
A&AEE	Aircraft and Armament Experimental Establishment		PSI or psi	Pounds per Square Inch
AB	Air Base		RAE	Royal Aircraft Establishment
AM	Air Ministry		RAF	Royal Air Force
ARI	Air Radio Installation		RAAF	Royal Australian Air Force
			RAN	Royal Australian Navy
CAG	Carrier Air Group		RATOG	Rocket Assisted Takeoff Gear
CAM	Catapult Armed Merchantman		RCAF	Royal Canadian Air Force
CAP	Combat Air Patrol		RCN	Royal Canadian Navy
			RCNAS	Royal Canadian Naval Air Station
DH	de Havilland		RFA	Royal Fleet Auxiliary
DTD	Directorate of Technical Development		RFC	Royal Flying Corps
			RN	Royal Navy
EAF	Egyptian Air Force		RNN	Royal Netherlands Navy (unofficial)
FAA	Fleet Air Arm		RNAS	Royal Naval Air Station
FAC	Fuerza Aerea de Cuba		RNVR	Royal Naval Volunteer Reserve
FAR	Fuerza Aerea Revolucionaria		RP	Rocket Projectile
FB	Fighter Bomber		RPM	Revolutions Per Minute
			R&R	Rest and Recuperation
HMS	His/Her Majesty's Ship			
HMAS	His/Her Majesty's Australian Ship		SAG	Support Air Group
HMCS	His/Her Majesty's Canadian Ship		SAR	Search And Rescue
HrMs	Her Majesty's Ship			
			UK	United Kingdom
ISS	Iraqi Single Seater		US	United States of America
IDT	Iraqi Dual Trainer		USAF	United States Air Force
			USMC	United States Marine Corps
MiG	Mikoyan and Gurevich		USN	United States Navy
MoS	Ministry of Supply		USS	United States Ship
NACA	National Advisory Committee on Aeronautics		VHF	Very High Frequency
NATO	North Atlantic Treaty Organization		ZBX	Radio Navigation Beacon

Unlimited Gold race line-up in front of the grandstands prior to the start of the 1999 Reno Air Races. This angle gives an excellent size comparison between the Sea Fury and the smaller P-51D. (Nicholas A. Veronico)

SIGNIFICANT DATES

1937
Specification F.118/37 issued to cover the development of the Tornado and Typhoon fighters.

6 October 1939
First flight of Vulture-engined prototype Tornado P5219.

24 February 1940
Initial flight of Centaurus Tornado HG441.

23 October 1941
Specification F.110/41 issued for Tempest as the Typhoon II.

2 September 1942
First flight of Tempest V HM593.

January 1943
Specification F.2/43 issued for the Tempest Lightweight fighter.

April 1943
Specification N.7/43 for naval fighter issued.

28 June 1943
Initial flight of Centaurus-powered Tempest II LA602.

1944
Specification N.22/43 issued for standard Fury for the Fleet Air Arm.

1 September 1944
Initial flight of Lightweight Fury prototype NX798.

21 February 1945
Maiden flight of Sea Fury prototype SR661.

12 October 1945
First flight of navalized Sea Fury prototype SR666.

7 September 1946
First flight of production Mk. X TF895 to Contract No. 3682/44 for 50 aircraft serialed TF895—TF928 and TF940-TF955.

12 October 1946
Royal Netherlands Navy orders 10 Sea Fury FB.50s to Contract N/SF/2001, followed by Contract N/SF/3001 for 12 aircraft, dated 12 January 1950

4 December 1946
Iraq orders 35 ISS single seaters and two ITS Fury aircraft for delivery during 1947–1948,

1947
Nos. 776, 802, 803, 805 and 807 Sqdrns equip with the Sea Fury Mk. X

July 1947
First flight of a production Sea Fury FB.11 to Contract No. 3682/44, aircraft serialed TF956-TF973 and TF985-TF999 plus TG113-TG129.

Second Contract No. 675/46, aircraft serialed VR918-VR952.

Third Contract No. 1584/47, aircraft serialed VW224-VW234, VW541-VW590, VW621-VW670, and VW714-VW718.

Fourth Contract No. 2576/48, aircraft serialed VX608-VX643, VX650-VX696, VX707-VX711, VX724-VX730, VX748-VX764, WF590-WF595, WF610-WF627.

Fifth Contract No. 3794/49, aircraft serialed WE673-WE694, WE708-WE736, WE785-WE806, WM742-WM482, and WM487-WM495.

Sixth Contract No. 5042/50, aircraft serialed WG564-WG575, WG590-WG604, and WG621-WG630.

Seventh Contract No. 5042/50, aircraft serialed WH581-WH594, WH612-WH623, WJ221-WJ248, WJ276-WJ292, and WJ294-WJ297 plus WJ299-WJ301.

Eighth Contract No. 6298/51, aircraft serialed WN474-WN479 and WN484-WN487.

Ninth Contract No. 7408/51, aircraft serialed WX627-WZ656.

15 January 1948
Initial flight of Sea Fury T.Mk. 20 prototype to Contract No. 1998/47.

Contract No. 1674/48, aircraft serialed VX280-VX292 and VX297-VX310.

Second Contract No. 2577/48, aircraft serialed VZ345-VX355 and VZ363-VZ372.

Third Contract No. 3794/49, aircraft serialed WE820-WE 826.

Fourth Contract No. 5042/50, aircraft serialed WG652-WG656.

May 1948
No. 802 Squadron is the first unit to receive the Sea Fury FB.11. To be followed by Nos. 801, 804, 805 and 807 Squadrons.

1949
Pakistani Air Force orders 143 fighter and fighter bombers under Contract 2795/49 for delivery during 1950.

1949
Egyptian Air Force orders twelve single seaters under Contract 17/49/USS.

November 1951
The RNVR receives the Sea Fury with Nos. 1831, 1832, 1833, 1834, 1835 and 1836 Squadrons equipping.

Mid 1953
The Sea Fury leaves FAA service.

1957
Union of Burma purchases 18 aircraft from the MoS under Contract HAL/57/B/030. Three trainers delivered under Contract HAL/57/B/030.

1957
Contract HAL/58/C/039 issued for Furies sold to Cuba for delivery in 1958.

1957
DLB orders reconditioned T.Mk. 20s for delivery during 1958–1960.